The Intelligent Investor's Mistakes:

Warren Buffett

38 Buffett's Investment Stories, Gain Wisdom, Master Risk, and Maximize Profits to Build Enduring Wealth

BALAJI KASAL

www.balajikasal.com

Copyright © 2024 by Balaji Kasal

Contact: info@balajikasal.com

On Mission @The Intelligent Investors Hub

www.intelligentinvestorshub.com

To my lovely family.

<u>May I Ask You a Favor?</u>

I would like to hear your thoughts about my book and book series – 'The Intelligent Investor's'. *Please leave a review on the platforms from you bought the book.*

It serves two purposes: first, it helps me understand what areas you want to master in the investment game, and second, it improves my craft for you.

Sincerely,

Thank You.

Balaji Kasal

<u>Your Free Gift!</u>

As a token of my ***thank you*** for taking out time to read the book and also for leaving a review.

Download your Free eBook pdf copy.

Alternatively, click:

https://balaji-kasal.ck.page/cb67feb275

Table of Content

Preface

This book was written to learn from the mistakes of the greatest investor, Warren Buffett. Let me declare at the beginning that he is one of the great heroes to me. Many books describe Buffett's success formulas, investment style, and life journey. The best concept in investing is to learn from other's mistakes rather than doing them ourselves!

I first encountered Buffett in 2005. I was on a start-up team after completing my post-graduation from IIT Bombay, a premier Technical Institute in India. Since then, I have started reading about and understanding him and Berkshire Hathaway Inc. (Berkshire). I read all his letters to the partners in his Buffett Partnership and later to Berkshire shareholders.

He inspired me to do an executive post-graduation program from the National Stock Exchange (NSE) and other certifications from the Bombay Stock Exchange (BSE) to learn about businesses and market ecosystems. And, of course, accounting, the language of business. In the same way, Charlie Munger inspired me not to pursue a full-time MBA, - 'invert', although I don't have an opinion against them.

I have been revisiting these letters recently. In a 1985 letter to Berkshire shareholders, Buffett acknowledged Charlie Munger, who advocated studying mistakes, rather than success, both in the business and other aspects of life. This inspired him to derive, *"All I want to know is where I'm going to die, so I'll never go there."*

In the same Chairman's letter, Buffett announced the *Shutdown of Textile Business*, saying he had generated *ample material to study his mistakes and errors.*

This inspired me to write this book!

*****

The major research for the book is from Buffett's letters, Berkshire's annual reports and Annual General Meetings, and his media interactions. I also studied the books and articles written about him. I apologize if you find any "errors". If so, kindly bring them to my notice with factual references to modify them, accordingly. *My Gratitude to you!*

These company stories run over years… and some cases over decades. Accounting practices have changed over this period. The data presented in Berkshire's annual report has changed too. I tried to be conscious while capturing them; I present them to you to make sense of them so the right message can be received. *As you know, facts matter in investments and businesses to make effective decisions. So in Life!*

In 2010, Todd Combs joined Berkshire as an investment manager, and a year later came Ted Weschler. They make independent investment decisions for Berkshire. So, if I did not get a correct reference for a transaction executed by Buffett himself, I skipped them in this book.

Please remember that the book was written in hindsight. Specific years are mentioned only for reference to put the story in perspective. Of course, a lot of events took place before and after. As you know, for an "investor" or a "businessman", these events occur on an ongoing basis.

I tried to avoid stock price movement discussions wherever possible. For me, the key messages are to learn about investment opportunities, business economics, and how to value them. The prices may deviate on either side to any extent for any given point of time. Benjamin Graham correctly pointed out, *"In the short run, the market is a voting machine but in the long run, it is a weighing machine."*

*****

The sequence of stories starts in 1965 when Buffett first acquired Berkshire Hathaway Inc., the event that transformed him. I believe what you are about to learn here will help you excel in the investment game.

The core focus of this book is to learn from an intelligent investor. Apart from the brief coverage of Buffett's investments, you will learn lessons to improve your toolkit. You should get an edge in finding opportunities and executing decisions while taking a perspective that makes the most sense to you.

I kept the book structure simple and crisp so you can learn quickly. I love short books with powerful ideas. Each chapter offers a brief story about the company or a business "group", where Buffett made a "mistake". It is followed by the quote(s) from Buffett, and bonus quote(s) from Munger associated with the company. The lessons and insights are mine as a key takeaway for you. There might be a possibility some lesson seems to repeat based on the story. However, *I believe that repetition and consistency help to develop a habit!*

Thank you.

Disclosure: *I do not hold any shares of Berkshire Hathaway Inc.*

Introduction

"I like to study failure. We want to see what has caused businesses to go bad, and the biggest thing that kills them is complacency. You want a restlessness, a feeling that somebody's always after you, but you're going to stay ahead of them. That restlessness — that tomorrow is more exciting than today — you have to have it permeate the organization." - Warren Buffett, 2013 at The Coca-Cola Company's AGM

Warren Buffett has a terrific record as an investor and businessman. Charlie Munger and he built Berkshire Hathaway Inc (Berkshire) from a textile company in 1965. Today, it is a holding company for businesses that they either fully or partially own. The market value of Berkshire nears $900 billion as of March 2024. It was the world's 8th most valuable company also in 2024. Berkshire has become a vehicle to ride for many people for their financial success.

Buffett started his investment journey at an early age when he was just eleven years old. Since childhood, he entertained many interesting projects, all entrepreneurial. He played many roles as a salesman, speculator, and trader. I believe these experiences shaped him. They helped him to build a strong foundation as a great investor, businessman, and legend.

Buffett **evolved** from a trader, investor, and businessman into an empire builder. The success he achieved is remarkable and unique in many ways. It is amazing to achieve this kind of success in one's lifetime. It puzzles me more, knowing the kind of mistakes made on the way. There are many mistakes, and a few are major. The big ones are omissions, not commissions. It means he did NOT buy the investments he liked and understood. I dedicated a complete section of the book to them.

Buffett openly confesses his mistakes and embraces them. *Mistakes are* inevitable *in investments.* Further, he acknowledges that he will be making more mistakes in the future. However, he mastered learning from his mistakes and moving forward. It is the key to success. These mistakes didn't hold him back. He understands the edges of his circle of competence.

There is another angle to embrace the mistakes is his *leadership style.* He encourages Berkshire business managers to report their issues and mistakes, promptly so the corrective actions may be expedited. This practice helps maintain Berkshire's reputation. *It is a corporate culture trait!*

In 1989, Buffett published, "Mistakes of the First Twenty-five Years", in Berkshire's annual shareholder letter. He reviewed his mistakes in that letter. I believe these confessions helped him to feel relieved. Also, in another 25 years, in 2015, he predicted there more pages to cover his mistakes (not published). Buffett expects more mistakes at Berkshire in the future. They will be of omission and not commission.

If you look at Buffett's investment journey, he kept evolving. He experimented with many things. H succeeded as shown in the records, and he also failed few times. He started as a cigar-butt investor; later, he became a successful businessman. He enjoyed the journey, and it kept him active. In fact, he has the longest record of successful investments. *This reflects his character trait to keep learning and evolve!*

This is quite different from his teacher's belief. Professor Benjamin Graham (Ben), retired from active investing at the age of 62, in 1956. Ben thought there were no challenges to solve in the investment world. He was more of a professor, challenge seeker, and problem solver.

*****

As noted, on his long journey, Buffett made many mistakes. They were of different types at different stages. They were in business acquisition, common stock investment, and in the trade. It is easier for an investor to correct a mistake in a marketable security. Just sell the stock either immediately, or in the near future, based on the assessment.

In the case of an owned business, fixing the mistake might be an ongoing activity... and it is hard. In some cases, let them run it on their own but with no more capital allocation. In most cases, the businesses need to be either liquidated or sold.

Buffett also made mistakes in accessing the economic characteristics of a business, like in the airline business. Sometimes, he traded in the commodity business when the cycle was at its peak. Like ConocoPhillips, an oil & gas exploration and production company. This is because humans are easily carried away in a booming market, as in 2007. A few mistakes involve not acting quickly enough, the effect of over-caution or procrastination. This caused him to miss out on a few wonderful opportunities. For example, Google.

Buffett and Munger together built a strong filtering mechanism in 'decision-making'. They were quick to say "no" most of the time. This behavior offended many people. Even then, they made many mistakes. These mistakes were due to Buffett's own biases and emotions. They include too much optimism and pessimism. In a few cases, he failed to do a holistic business analysis and recognize the economic outcome. The mistakes are both of omission as well as in commission categories.

Despite these mistakes, Buffett and Munger built a business empire from scratch. They were open and honest about their mistakes. They were learning machines. They used these experiences to improve their investment approach over time.

As an investor, mistakes are eminent on the journey. The trick is to recognize them promptly and do something about them; that is what matters, and the sooner is better. With this, you can turn, *lemons into lemonade.* Unfortunately, in the investment world, the rear-view mirror is always clearer than the windshield.

My major intent is to capture learnings from Buffett's mistakes to help you become a successful investor. Of course, they could be helpful for a trader, as well. On my own journey, I made a lot of mistakes as part of a reasonable record in life. But recognizing them and correcting them promptly matters the most... no matter what it takes. It needs not only humility and a strong gut, but *character!* Amazon founder, Jeffrey Bezos, says he is not defensive and wants to learn from his failures. *Grow through adversity.*

Mistakes impart wisdom on what not to do. Of course. I prefer to learn from others than my own experiences. This book is my attempt to study mistakes and present them as learnings to you. I believe they will help you to become a successful investor and live a fulfilled life.

Have a Joyful Journey!

<u>PART-A</u>: Mistakes of Commission

"The man who does things makes mistakes, but he doesn't make the biggest mistake of all-doing nothing." -Benjamin Franklin

Chapter 1: Berkshire Hathaway Inc.

[Year- 1965]

"Emotions are more spontaneous than thoughts." - Shri Ramakrishna Paramahansa

Berkshire and Hathaway were two age-old textile companies that merged in 1955. It was the only surviving textile company in New England. The company had fifteen operating plants with over $120 million in revenue. By 1962, Berkshire Hathaway Inc.'s (Berkshire's) scale of operation had shrunk to only seven operating plants. The company was making losses. The stock market valued the company at only $7.50 per share, while the working capital was $10.25, and the book value was $20.20.

Buffett was aware of the company while working at Graham-Newman Corp. The company was co-founded by Benjamin Graham. During this time in 1962, Buffett was managing funds for a group of people he knew. The Buffett Partnership Ltd. (BPL) was making returns well above the Dow Jones Industrial Average, as well as many leading investment firms at that time.

Considering the market price, Buffett found it a typical cigar-butt value investment opportunity. Buffett started buying Berkshire at $7.50 per share in December of 1962. He did this under the "Private Owner" category of the BPL. Under this category, Buffett generally purchased undervalued stocks.

In Berkshire's purchase, the main qualification for Buffett was its bargain price. It is a typical Benjamin Graham value teaching. It was selling well below working capital, although it showed a significant net loss over the last ten years. There were expectations in the market that the company could buy back the share in the future. Buffett felt he could tender the shares in the company's buy-back process at a higher price and make a good gain on the deal. So, the investment thesis was clear: buy-in, as cigar-butt value investing, and sell out or tender the shares whenever the opportunity arises.

Seabury Stanton was the president of Berkshire, in charge of the overall operations of Berkshire operations. In 1964, as expected, promoters planned to buy back the shares. As Buffett Partnership was holding a big chunk of stock, Stanton enquired Buffett for a price at which he could tender them. As per Buffett's calculations, the fair price was $11.50 per share. Mr Stanton agreed to the same price.

However, when the offer letter was received on 6th May 1964, the tender ask price was $11.375 per share, $1/8 less. Buffett was furious and felt cheated. He was carried away emotionally;

instead of selling the shares, he started buying Berkshire shares.

One reason for Buffett's unusual behaviour was Howard Buffett, Warren's father. He died six days before the tender offer on April 30, 1964. Buffett regarded his father as a hero and was very close to him. Buffett might have been going through a depression. He might not had the right frame of mind essential for a rational decision.

By April 1965, Buffett and BPL, the partnership firm, became major shareholders of Berkshire. BPL partners' holding was more than 38% stake, which accounted for more than 25% of the partnership's total capital. Till then Buffett maintained secrecy by showing holdings under the broker's account.

In early May 1965, during the board meeting, BPL formally took control of Berkshire. Stanton resigned from the board. Buffett was appointed as Chairman and since then has been running the Berkshire business. When BPL took control, Berkshire operations had already been scaled down to only two mills and 2,300 employees.

Buffett knew that the textile business could not be profitable. However, he felt comfortable owning the mills. He was betting on the newly appointed President, Kenneth Chace, and other salespeople in Berkshire. Also, one of the

reasons Buffett gave to BPL partners in his letter
was that there were no labor unions in southern
textile plants. Hence, he believed it could be an
important competitive advantage.

Chace was in charge of all the operations at
Berkshire, while Buffett took charge of capital
allocation. Buffett asked Chace to run the
operations with no or minimal new capital. He
asked him to send monthly financial statements
to him at Omaha. Over the next two years, textile
operations turned profitable. In 1967, Buffett
declared only the maiden dividend of 10 cents
per share in the history of Berkshire, since he
took the charge.

However, soon after, the textile business started
struggling to survive. Working capital and labor-
intensive businesses demanded more capital
from Buffett. Further, the high electricity
expenses added more challenges. A commodity
textile business was competing in a global
marketplace. During the next twenty years,
textile operations were doing either losses or
barely able to generate mediocre returns. It was
always one step forward, and two steps back
scenario.

Meanwhile, in 1969, Buffett dissolved his
partnership. He became the full-time Chairman
of Berkshire Hathaway Inc. Later in the 1983
annual report, Buffett confessed, *"The book
value consists of textile assets that could not*

earn, on average, anything close to an appropriate rate of return. In terms of our analogy, the investment in textile assets resembled investment in a largely wasted education."

Buffett cites one reason for keeping the textile division for twenty years: it was the labor at the operations. He tried to sell it off to other companies, but that didn't work out. Finally, after twenty years post-acquisition of Berkshire Hathaway, Buffett decided to close down the textile division in July 1985.

*****

The good part of this whole episode was that Buffett maintained tight control over the capital allocation to the textile business. It helped to limit the capital drain, and the surplus capital was utilized in acquiring other businesses. So, the impact of textile business operations was shrinking over this period for Berkshire.

Buffett started "diversification: as early as in 1966. He and his friends, Charlie Munger and David Gottesman, bought a company called, Hochschild Kohn, in Baltimore, Maryland. It was a department store. However, the company disappeared over time. We will talk about it later in the book.

In 1967, when Berkshire made a profit and generated cash, Buffett purchased National Indemnity Insurance Company. This was a "colossal" mistake, to be discussed later. However, it gave Berkshire an entry into insurance. Later, the insurance division's cash (float) became the core engine for buying other wonderful businesses for Berkshire.

During this period, Buffett and Munger were managing three businesses separately. They were the majority shareholders and decided to merge them together: Diversified Retailing, Blue Chip Stamps, and Berkshire. This gave Berkshire Hathaway Inc. today's avatar. Based on Munger's guidance, Buffett started focusing more on purchasing wonderful businesses to grow Berkshire: insurance businesses, marketable securities, and controlling companies.

———

In Buffett's own words [1985 AR]:
"When a management with a reputation for brilliance tackles a business with a reputation for poor fundamental economics, it is the reputation of the business that remains intact... Should you find yourself in a chronically leaking boat, energy devoted to changing vessels is likely to be more productive than energy devoted to patching leaks."

Lessons:

1. An investor needs to be close to the matter to be rational. The facts matter rather than being carried away by emotions. The market doesn't know about either your feelings or emotions.

2. The key to investing is to understand why something is "cheaply" available. Is It really an opportunity for long term journey or just a cigar-butt?

3. The cigar-butt investment style has a classic challenge. It looks only at the gap between market price and intrinsic value and misses the big picture. It's a short-sighted approach that might work in trading marketable securities; however, not as a long-term investor or as a business owner. To gain long term, you need to know the business's economic traits.

4. Investors need to remain agile and recognize their circle of competence. They need to book losses or bad investments as quickly as possible. It not only frees up capital but also the mental capital to focus on other better investment opportunities. In the span of twenty years, Buffett recognized that the textile business would not generate high

returns on investments. However, he delayed and hoped for a reasonable return.

5. If the investor's thesis has broken, she or he should reevaluate the scenarios and plan to sell sooner rather than later to free-up the resources.

Chapter 2: Waumbec Textile Company
[Year- 1975]

1+1=2 May not True in Business

In April of 1975, Berkshire acquired loss-making Waumbec Mills Inc. and Waumbec Dyeing & Finishing Co. Inc., located in Manchester, New Hampshire. These companies were engaged in manufacturing, distributing, and selling finished woven fabrics. The deal was to buy these businesses for $1.6 million cash. Plus, Berkshire was to pay 8% annual interest on the outstanding principal loan of $1.15 million.

Buffett acquired Waumbec as a bargain: He based the purchase on its assets, projected fit with his business, and some tax benefits from past losses. We expected Berkshire's productivity to get a boost at Manchester. This would happen in the weaving and finishing areas, using Waumbec's facility. On the other hand, Waumbec would market its own products effectively in areas where Berkshire had strength. Also, Waumbec drapery material complements Berkshire products and could be marketed through Berkshire owned Home Fabrics Division.

The textile division kept dragging down Berkshire's performance. This continued for ten years until the operations closed in 1985. Buffett had recognized the low returns earned by the textile business. Also, many Berkshire shareholders questioned the rationale for sticking to the textile business.

———

In Buffett's own words [2014 AR]: "Nevertheless – surprise, surprise – Waumbec was a disaster, with the mill having to be closed down not many years later." … "Time is the *friend of the wonderful business, the enemy of the mediocre.*"

Lessons:

1. The commodity businesses' consolidation and synergy strategies fail faster to historic average or below. Here, 1+1 is less than 2.

2. Cigar-butt value investing is a trading strategy. However, if you are investing for the long-term, you need to avoid them for three reasons. First, they eat up capital. Second, the time to realize the gain is unknown. Third, holding them burns out investor's mental resources and other better opportunities.

3. It is always a wise idea to correct a
    mistake as early as possible rather than
    hoping for better days.

Chapter 3: Hochschild Kohn & Co.
[Year - 1966]

"You have to be merchandise driven. Otherwise, you become like everybody else."
\- Sam M. Walton

Soon after acquiring Berkshire in 1966, Buffett acquired Hochschild Kohn (HK). It was a privately held departmental store located at Baltimore. At that time, he was running Buffett Partnership Ltd.(BPL) He acquired an 80% stake in the store through BPL controlled Diversified Retailing operations, while Charlie Munger and David Gottesman took 10% each. This was the first time both Buffett and Munger together had carried out an acquisition.

To purchase the store, Buffett and Munger both tried to seek a loan. However, the Manager declined it, saying "Six million for a small and old store?" Even then, both did not question their own judgment and acquisition rationale. Buffett made the deal at a substantial discount from book value. HK also had some real-estate properties. The HK store was run by Louis Kohn with whom Buffett used to socialize.

The retailing was highly competitive around the Baltimore area. The store was running on a thin margin. Further, Kohn was planning to expand the stores to nearby regions. Buffett and Munger know it would be challenging to operate in these regions. HK needs to compete with small retail stores. Luckily, after three years, in 1969 Buffett was able to sell barely at the purchase price. However, in this episode, both Buffett and Munger learned what goes into a retail business operation and how to run it.

———

Buffett's own words [1998 AGM]:
"We've made bad — lots of bad deals. We made a bad deal when we bought Hochschild Kohn, for example, the department store operation, back in 1966. But it had — fine people — but we were wrong on the economics of the business."

Bonus: Munger's own words:
"Buying Hochschild-Kohn was like the story of a man who buys a yacht. The two happy days are the day he buys it and the day he sells it."

Lessons:

1. A business owner needs to evaluate its sustainable competitive strength to operate and produce profits.

2. Merely engaging in an acquisition solely based on asset price lacks a rationale,

unless the acquisition is pursued with the intention to liquidate for profit.

Chapter 4: National Indemnity Company
[Year - 1967]

Ownership Structure Decides Economic Gain.

National Indemnity Company (NICO) was a small insurer based out of Omaha where Warren Buffett lives. Jack Ringwalt, the owner, was Buffett's friend. He wanted to sell the company only to Buffett. Buffett liked the insurance business and had a sweet spot for it.

In 1967, Buffett was running his partnership (BPL) while also running Berkshire. He could have purchased National Indemnity under the partnership. If so, he and his partners could have owned 100% of this wonderful business. Also, he could have consolidated future business acquisitions under BPL. This would have given 100% ownership to Buffett and BPL partners.

However, Buffett bought NICO from Berkshire's capital for $8.6 million. Because of this transaction, BPL and Buffett owned only 61% stake in NICO. Legacy shareholders of Berkshire owned the remaining 39%. This single "event" eventually diverted hundreds of billions from known BPL partners to unknown people.

This was the biggest mistake for Buffett himself and BPL partners. On the plus side, however,

Buffett got a public platform through Berkshire. He used it to express his investment thesis, helping him to take on the world stage. The new platform was more impactful as a public figure.

Later, Buffett admitted his mistake of selecting the wrong vehicle to buy wonderful businesses. He kept investing by acquiring businesses either fully or partially through Berkshire. Later, he merged Berkshire with Diversified Retailing and Blue Chip Stamps, as described earlier. Starting to build an empire under Berkshire Hathaway Inc. was "accidental" as Buffett did not know exactly why.

———

Buffett's own words [2014 AR]:
"So why did I purchase NICO for Berkshire rather than for BPL? I've had 48 years to think about that question, and I've yet to come up with a good answer. I simply made a colossal mistake... I opted to marry 100% of an excellent business (NICO) to a 61%-owned terrible business (Berkshire Hathaway), a decision that eventually diverted $100 billion or so from BPL partners to a collection of strangers."

Lessons:

1. Ownership and capital structure are the starting point for any investment

journey. The percentage of your holding in a business decides the long-term economic benefits you gain from it.

2. Once you pick up an investment vehicle, changing later can be expensive and hard. So, plan capital structure and allocation with an eye to future plans to maximize the gains.

Chapter 5: The Walt Disney Company
[Years – 1966, and 2001]

A Repeat Mistake.

Disney is a multinational mass media and entertainment conglomerate, based in Burbank, California. The company was founded by brothers, Walt Disney and Roy Disney in 1923. It is known for animations, live-action films, television productions and theme parks. The company kept growing by expanding its own businesses and through acquisitions. Now, it ranked among the top 100 on Fortune's list of largest US companies in terms of revenue.

In 1965, Buffett invested in Disney for his BPL partnership, following a "scuttlebutt" investment approach. Buffett flew to California to meet Mr. Disney, now in mid-60s. He was kind enough to explain his whole business plan to the thirty-five-year-old visitor, Buffett. Later he visited Disney's movie theatre to get a sense of the company's popularity. He viewed the Disney business prospects and found the company to be a value buy.

Buffett purchased a 5% stake in Disney for $4 million. In 1965, the company earned $21 million pre-tax with cash on books and was valued at around $80 million. However, after a year, Buffett sold out the stake for $6 million and pocketed a healthy 50% profit for BPL.

Buffett had been well aware of the Disney's popularity as a brand. Since the beginning, Disney enjoyed the mind share of the masses. It pioneered animation and theme park industries. The brand pull was such that any parent would shell out extra dollars for their kids' entertainment. Kids were in safe hands around the Disney brand and ecosystem. This pricing power of Disney was evident at its theme parks and for its proprietary content. Multiple revenue streams and brands offered a sustained long-term competitive advantage.

However, Buffett was a follower of his guru, Benjamin Graham, who advocated cigar-butt value investing. That might be why Buffett sold Disney and pocketed a 50% gain. He ignored the long-term compounding of this wonderful business.

Again after thirty years, in 1995, opportunity knocked for Buffett and Berkshire. Disney wanted to merge with Capital Cities/ABC Inc. Berkshire had a stake in Capital Cities. (I will describe the details about the mistakes in Capital Cities later in the chapter.) When Capital Cities got merged into Disney, Berkshire got $1.4 billion in cash and a 3.6% stake in Disney. However, in 2001, Buffett sold his complete stake in Disney.

If Buffett had kept these stakes until now, they would be valued at $8 billion today, excluding all the dividends paid by Disney over this period. Sometimes, Buffett tries to justify these mistakes. He could have diverted the capital to buy other wonderful businesses like Coca-Cola.

The dominance of technology and competition might have driven selling in 2001. During the dot-com boom, Disney planned to enter the technology and internet businesses. Buffett might have felt uncomfortable and had seen challenges for the business. Buffett made a mistake *twice* in the case of Disney because of his short-sightedness.

———

Buffett's own words [1998 AGM, Et al.]:

*"You don't have to be a financial analyst, you don't have to be finance major, to know that $80m is a ridiculous valuation. Eleven million people a year go to Disneyland. That's $7 a person [or $77m a year] and you get [the rest of the company] thrown in free. It was a joke." …"
It's good to learn from your mistakes. It's better to learn from other people's mistakes." … "And certainly the Disney sale in the '60s was a huge mistake. I should have been buying, forget about holding, and selling."*

Bonus: Munger's own words [1996 AGM]:

"... I don't know about your children and grandchildren, but mine want to see Disney. And they want to see it... over and over and over again. They don't want to see Katzenberg."

Lessons:

1. Long-term compounding in wonderful businesses works like magic. So, sit tight on them. Conversely, selling wonderful business too soon is a mistake.

2. Before making any investment decision, specifically on selling, weigh it critically Here you are juggling among potential business prospectus, market scenarios, and opportunity costs. Hence selling is tricky in the investment business.

3. Selling makes sense if the original reason to buy is no longer valid. This could be due to fundamental challenges in business growth. Or, the share price might have risen unrealistically high, and *valuations* are not justified. Or, you might get a better opportunity.

Chapter 6: Capital Cities/ABC Inc.

[Year - 1991]

No Investment so Permanent.

Capital Cities/ABC Inc. was formed in 1985 when Capital Cities Communications purchased the American Broadcasting Company (ABC). Capital Cities paid $3.5 billion for the acquisition. It was the largest non-oil deal at that time in the business history. Buffett financed the deal and in turn, got a 25% stake in the merged entity for $515 million.

Capital Cities/ABC owned many radio and television stations across the US. The company is also in the newspaper and magazine publishing business. Tom Murphy and Daniel Burke were running the operations. Buffett had high regard for and belief in the team. Buffett said, "Probably the greatest two-person combination in management that the world has ever seen or maybe ever will see."

In 1986, Capital Cities/ABC was a top holding in the Berkshire Hathaway. In the annual report, Buffett proclaimed that Capital Cities would be part of the permanent holdings, along with GEICO and Washington Post. Within five years, in 1991, Buffett realized that media businesses were facing a secular transformation. This was the time when the Internet was spreading its wings as a delivery platform. Buffett saw the challenges: media businesses becoming more segmented and their earning power declining

In 1993, Buffett cut the holding in Capital Cities/ABC by one-third. Berkshire made a $297 million post-tax gain after holding them for eight years. Later in 1995, Capital Cities/ABC merged with the Walt Disney Company.

———

Buffett's own *words [1986 AR]:*
"We should note that we expect to keep permanently our three primary holdings, Capital Cities/ABC, Inc., GEICO Corporation, and The Washington Post. Even if these securities were to appear significantly overpriced, we would not anticipate selling them, just as we would not sell See's or Buffalo Evening News if someone were to offer us a price far above what we believe those businesses are worth."

[1991 AR]: "The economic strength of once-mighty media enterprises continues to erode as retailing patterns change and advertising and entertainment choices proliferate. In the business world, unfortunately, the rear-view mirror is always clearer than the windshield."

[1994 AR]: *"Late in 1993 I sold 10 million shares of Cap Cities at $63; at year-end 1994, the price was $85.25. (The difference is $222.5 million for those of you who wish to avoid the pain of calculating the damage yourself.) When we purchased the stock at $172.5 in 1986, I told you that I had previously sold our Cap Cities holdings at $43 per share during 1978-80 and added that I was at a loss to explain my earlier behavior. Now I've become a repeat offender. Maybe it's time to get a guardian appointed."*

Lessons:

1. An investor's job is not only to buy and hold but also to track the business and industry prospects. The opportunity cost to hold or sell could be better decision criteria, rather than "permanence'"

2. The permanent investment holding is *a myth*. The world is changing faster than ever. Businesses have faced consistent challenges from technological innovations and changes in customer preferences.

Chapter 7: Nebraska Furniture Mart:
[Year – 1983]

A Formal Contract Matters.

Nebraska Furniture Mart (NFM) is a home furnishing store located in Omaha, Nebraska. The products sold by the company include furniture, flooring, appliances, and electronics. Rose Blumkin (Mrs. B), a migrant woman, had started a small furniture store in 1937. She had a humble beginning with an initial capital of $500 from her brother.

She had no schooling or any formal education. She grew the business over decades. The key to her success was to offer better deals to the customers. This delighted them, and by 1983, she had grown the store to 200,000 square feet. While the sales were $100 million from this single location, the earnings before tax were $3.8 million.

In 1983, when Mrs. B turned 89, Buffett acquired an 80% stake in NFM for $60 million. They did it with a one-page handshake deal. Buffett praised Mrs. B for her business acumen. But in 1989, Mrs. B and her family/management had a disagreement over the remodeling of the operations of the carpet division. It was losing the stream. As no consensus was reached, she quit NFM.

Within a few months, at the age of 96, she started a new store, Mrs. B's Clearance and Factory Outlet bang opposite NFM. She was selling carpets and furniture. Within three years of operation, the store grew to become the third largest store in Omaha. It also became profitable — *a unique case of the entrepreneurial spirit!*

While NFM, Berkshire's subsidiary, was losing business; the pre-tax profit reported $17.1 million in 1989 dropped to $14.4 million in 1991. In 1991, Mrs. B decided to sell her new store to Berkshire. It merged with NFM. This time, Buffett made sure to get a non-competitive agreement signed. NFM business was back on track and growing again. In 1992, NFM's pre-tax profit was back to $17.1 million.

Mrs. B continued to run her new store until the age of 103. In 1998, she died at 104.

——

Buffett's own words [1992 AR]:

"Her business story has no parallel and I have always been a fan of hers, whether she was a partner or a competitor. But believe me, partner is better… this time around, Mrs. B graciously offered to sign a noncompete

agreement - and I, having been incautious on this point when she was 89, snapped at the deal. Mrs. B belongs in the Guinness Book of World Records on many counts. Signing a non-compete at 99 merely adds one more."

Lessons:

1. A well-drafted formal contract helps in any business deal, to avoid any unforeseen and unpleasant surprises in the future.

2. The promoter(s) and their family dynamics make a lot of difference for a family run business. It decides not only the business' fate, but also the shareholders' treatment.

Chapter 8: World Book Inc.
[Year 1985]

Technology Makes All the Difference.

In early 1986, Buffett bought Scott & Fetzer Company for $315 million. It had a book value of $173 million. He paid $142 million as goodwill (a premium).

Scott & Fetzer ran seventeen businesses, with a total revenue of $700 million. The major reason for the acquisition was its subsidiary, World Book Inc. The company was a dominant player in publishing printed encyclopedia books in the US, and it was the top revenue contributor to the group at 40%.

Buffett and Munger both had a personal connection to the product. They saw it as a "special" product. While other units suffered losses, Buffett decided to buy the Scott & Fetzer group. World Book kept growing for the next few years; Buffett was applauding the business growth when the revenue peaked at $31.8 million in 1991.

However, since then, the company started losing business, and revenue plunged to $8.8 million in 1995. The business took a toll against newer ways of delivery of the product: CD-ROM and online offerings. Microsoft launched Encarta, a digital encyclopedia in 1993 that became popular in no time.

World Book was facing stiff competition and challenges from new forms of competition. Buffett was optimistic about its business revamp. Management started to invest heavily in electronic products to stay relevant, and they started optimizing the overhead costs. These efforts were expected to improve the viability of the business. However, World Book's business failed to compete and sustain the company.

World Book's last reported pre-tax earnings was $12.6 million in the 1996 Berkshire annual report. It was somewhat improved from the previous year at which time it was reported as $8.8 million.

———

Buffett's own words [1995 AR]:

"Berkshire's most difficult problem is World Book, which operates in an industry beset by increasingly tough competition from CD-ROM and on-line offerings."

[1996 AGM]: *"And I don't think it (World Book) will be the business that it was five years ago, because the world is changed in some ways on that."*

Lessons:

1. Personal computers and the Internet changed the world and the way businesses operate since the 1990s. This was a titanic shift in world order. In investing, one must recognize disruptions and handle their affairs well.

2. New technologies are bringing rapid changes to the world and to businesses. An investor's job is getting harder to identify the businesses with lasting competitive advantages.

3. Shying away from understanding newer technology and its impact on business is no longer an option in this era. To stay and grow in the investment game, you need to keep learning and act based on newer facts.

Chapter 9: USAir Group Inc.
[Years – 1989, and 2020]

Unregulated Commodity.

The du Pont family founded USAir way back in 1939. We can trace its roots to that time. By 1989, it was operating many routes across the US. Buffett negotiated the purchase. He bought $358 million in preferential shares of USAir Group in 1989. The deal gave Berkshire a 9.25% annual dividend to redeem in ten years. Also, it bestowed rights to convert shares into common stock at a fixed price of $60 per share.

Buffett was bullish on the airline; he saw its potential to make money. He failed to evaluate all aspects of the airline as an investment. Buffett's thesis was to lend money to USAir and earn a fixed income. Meanwhile, he would get an equity conversion option.

As soon as Berkshire checked in, the airline started an uncontrolled descent. All the business and industry problems started to appear. The situation got worse for USAir when Piedmont Airlines Inc. merged with it in the same year. Buffett was well aware of merger issues, although he had not accounted for them in his evaluation.

As you know, an airline seat is a commodity, and other carriers fight to get it filled up by bidding at lower prices. An airline does not have any edge in an unregulated market.

Buffett missed out on calculating the capital-intensive nature of the airline business. The main costs for airline business operations are plane maintenance, fuel, and the crew.

To grow the business, they need to spend capital on aircraft. They also need to bid for more profitable routes and prime time slots. Just standing an aircraft at an airport adds to the cost. These huge costs put airlines at risk of bankruptcy. They need to generate consistent and sufficient revenue to sustain operations.

These multiple issues dropped Berkshire's value of investment in USAir to $215 million in 1995. Luckily, CEO Stephen Wolf rescued the company from the brink of bankruptcy. That made Berkshire recover the principal amount and dividends.

*****

Fast forward to 2016 and Berkshire bought into the top four US airlines: Delta Airways Inc., Southwest Airlines Inc., United Continental Holding Inc., and American Airlines Group Inc. Berkshire had one of the largest holdings. Buffett was following the "basket" investment approach, where you purchase the most influential players in the industry. It is like getting a monopoly by owning multiple companies in the same industry.

As per the 2019 annual report, these holdings increased in market value. Also, Berkshire received proportionate dividends during the holding period. However, records show that these holdings were sold by mid-2020 when the COVID-19 pandemic hit the airline business hard. They suffered and reported losses. The exact gain/loss for Berkshire was not mentioned in the annual report. Also, it was not clear who had made these investments. As of now, along with Buffett, Berkshire has other Investment Managers.

PS: As per news articles, some investments were by other Investment Managers (s) at Berkshire. However, major purchases were made by Buffett.

———

Buffett's own words [1994 AR]:

"Top honors go to a mistake I made five years ago that fully ripened in 1994: Our $358 million purchase of USAir preferred stock, on which the dividend was suspended in September. In the 1990 Annual Report I correctly described this deal as an "unforced error," meaning that I was

neither pushed into the investment nor misled by anyone when making it. Rather, this was a case of sloppy analysis, a lapse that may have been caused by the fact that we were buying a senior security or by hubris. Whatever the reason, the mistake was large." ...

"The worst sort of business is one that grows rapidly, requires significant capital to engender the growth, and then earns little or no money. Think airlines. Here a durable competitive advantage has proven elusive ever since the days of the Wright Brothers."..."

Bonus: Munger's own words:

"The airline experience was very unpleasant for us... We try and learn from those experiences but we're very slow learners. "

Lessons:

1. The insight into the nature of business is crucial for investment. A more critical approach to the margin of safety is needed for commodities like businesses.

2. For long-term investment success, you need to look for a lasting competitive edge.

3. I see many investors become carried away by sales growth (top-line). However, investors and smart businessmen need to *demand* growing retained earnings.

4. The cost analysis to run a business is part of the basic hygiene check. The real test is the requirement for external capital to grow.

Chapter 10: Salomon Brothers Inc.

[Year – 1991]

"It takes many good deeds to build a good reputation, and only one bad one to lose it." - Benjamin Franklin

In the 1980's, Buffett was fond of negotiated purchases. He used to apply for preferred shares since they gave a fixed return over time. In the end, they offered the option to convert to common stock. This was one of his favorite investment strategies, and he used it repeatedly over the period. In 1987, Buffett bought 9% preferred stock from Salomon Brothers Inc. for $700 million. The deal was with an option to convert into common stocks at $38 per share after three years. If not converted, it would be redeemable rateably over five years beginning in 1995.

He viewed this investment as a medium-term fixed-income security with an option to convert to common stocks. The investment theme was Salomon's leading position on Wall Street, and the most profitable bank. Salomon used to raise considerable capital for clients to execute market-making operations. They were minting money and generating a good return on equity. Buffett wanted to take advantage Salomon's position; he was expecting more value in future rights conversion.

He knew the investment business was less predictable than other businesses owned by Berkshire. He also said that he lacked insight into this investment's outcome. Buffett and Munger both praised Salomon CEO John Gutfreund for his honesty. They also praised his ability to run investment banking. They have known him since 1976. He helped to rescue GEICO from near bankruptcy.

There was a turn for the Salomon in 1991, when a rough trader bid more than the limit set by the US Treasury. The management and Gutfreund failed to report this misconduct to the US Treasury. The same rough trader made the mistake again in the next few days. This time, the US Treasury Department caught Salomon. They were furious about not reporting to them on time and escaping the disciplinary action.

The US government prosecuted Salomon for false submission of bids to manipulate the market. Salomon was suspended from joining the government bond auction. They were also fined heavily, which brought Salomon to the verge of bankruptcy.

Buffett and Munger were on the board of Salomon. They promptly joined the action.

Buffett knew it would be disastrous not only for Salomon but for Wall Street as well.

Salomon's board nominated Buffett as Interim-Chairman. Buffett gave the SEC all the documents. The SEC used them to investigate the issue until they were satisfied. Buffett convinced the U.S. Treasury to reverse the order and allow Salomon to bid in bond auctions. The U.S. Treasurer trusted Buffett because of Buffett's reputation. Finally, in 1992, Salomon was rescued with a $290 million fine.

Later, Buffett hired a new head at Salomon to place things in order.

In 1997, Salomon merged into Traveler Group. Berkshire sold its holding and made twice the money. However, the Salomon episode cost Buffett and Munger time and agitation. Further, a non-reversible reputation was at stake. The indirect cost to Buffett and Berkshire was much more than they had earned from the profits.

Salomon was operating in a complex Wall Street world. Both Buffett and Munger acknowledged later that the investment in Salomon had been a mistake.

———

Buffett's own words:

[1991, Testimony Salomon Brothers, Security Trading Investigation, Reference: https://www.youtube.com/watch?v=MtaeGt3KwuA]

"If they follow this test, they need not fear my other message to them: Lose money for the firm, and I will be understanding; lose a shred of reputation for the firm, and I will be ruthless."

[1994 AGM]:

"Salomon, I think, is a better company now than it was some years back. But it's still in a business that's — can be very volatile, and it has a small amount — as does any investment banking firm and as any commercial banking firm — of systemic risk. I mean, you can't get rid of that."

Munger's own words [1996 AGM]:

"Salomon's earnings have always been volatile, at least all the time I've been around the place. And I don't think that that volatility will — is likely to disappear."

[2006 AGM]: *"So he (Nick Brady, US Treasurer) knew about us, and I think he trusted you, Warren. And I think that mattered that day. So these old-fashioned reputational."*

Lessons:

1. In the financial world, ***trust*** is most important in any transaction. It cultivates creditability and a lifelong reputation. An investor needs to demand from the people who are running the business. My grandmother used to say *that earning a reputation takes a lifetime, but you can lose it in a moment.*

2. It is wise to avoid an investment if you do not have insight into the future business prospects and profitability. Hence, need an edge.

3. Even if you trust the management based on past behavior, you need to be vigilant about their affairs.

Chapter 11: Dexter Shoe Company
[Year – 1993]

Equity is Priceless.

Dexter was a popularly priced shoe company, making shoes for men and women. It was run by Harold Alfond, the founder, and his nephew, Peter Lunder. The company was producing 7.5 million pairs of shoes annually in 1993.

Both Buffett and Munger endorsed the business. They also endorsed the people running it. They knew the US shoe industry was in decline due to competition from cheap-producing countries. However, they relied on management to keep competition at bay.

Buffett issued 25,203 Class-A shares of Berkshire valued at $443 million at the time then for the acquisition of Dexter. (You can easily calculate today's value.)

In earlier years, Buffett had bought two companies: H.H. Brown and Lowell Shoes, and had tasted some success. Buffett was bullish on the prospects of the shoe business. He was so carried away that he used to sing, "There's no business like the shoe business," as he drove to work.

He planned strategies around shoe businesses as a group in Berkshire. He assessed that the business had a durable competitive advantage. The shoe group's revenue and profits declined continuously since then, except in the year 1997. However, Buffett was in a denial-bias mood. He informed Berkshire shareholders that the setback was temporary — a cyclical problem, rather than a secular one.

By 1999, reports stated that 93% of the 1.3 billion pairs of shoes bought in the US came from abroad. The local shoe industry was not able to manage production and compete with lower-cost producers. The managers at Berkshire tried many operational changes to revive the shoe group's prospects. One major change was to procure shoes abroad. However, the cost kept going up.

Later, in 2001 and 2002, in annual letters, Buffett admitted the mistake. 1) buying Dexter 2) paying for it in exchange for Berkshire shares, and 3) procrastinating when he needed to change the operations. In 2001, the annual report dropped the shoe group. It put it under Other Businesses. He still had some hope for a revival. It would come in later years after several manager changes. He expected to earn a good return in the future, but nothing was specifically reported about it later.

Buffett failed to poise Dexter's business model strength against low-cost shoe producers and imports. The shoe business's low-cost moat vanished sooner than later. Buffett relied heavily on recent successes, rather than looking into future prospects. He overestimated the future earnings from an unregulated commodity like shoes.

The mistake at Berkshire was worse due to the issuing of Class-A shares, which cost 1.6% of Berkshire's net worth. This investment cost shareholders billions of dollars.

———

Buffett's own words [2007 AGM]:
"I made an even worse mistake when I said "yes" to Dexter, a shoe business I bought in 1993 for $433 million in Berkshire stock (25,203 shares of A). What I had assessed as durable competitive advantage vanished within a few years. But that's just the beginning: By using Berkshire stock, I compounded this error hugely. That move made the cost to Berkshire shareholders not $400 million, but rather $3.5 billion.
In essence, I gave away 1.6% of a wonderful business – one now valued at $220 billion – to buy a worthless business. To date, Dexter is the worst deal that I've made. But I'll make more mistakes in the future – you can bet on that. "...

"As a financial disaster, this one deserves a spot in the Guinness Book of World Records."

Lessons:

1. In a global scenario where goods can be moved easily across borders, it makes competition more severe where everyone seeks low-cost opportunities. This is far truer for unregulated commodity businesses.

2. Overconfidence and the thrill of past successes are the enemy of an investor.

3. In the long run, equity is always costly compared to cash. Hence, as an investor, you need to have a sharp focus on the issuance of shares in different forms: ESOPs, Warrants, Preferential, and Share swaps in acquisitions. These will dilute your ownership and per-share business value. Hence, these share offers need to be analysed critically and weighted against future prospectus. I avoided many companies where negligence occurs in share issuance.

Chapter 12: McDonald's Corporation

[Year – 1996]

*"We are not technically in the food business.
We in the real estate business."*
– Ray Croc, former CEO of McDonald's

McDonald's is a multinational fast food chain giant founded in 1940. It is the world's largest fast-food chain, serving more than 40,000 outlets in more than 100 countries. It enjoys the sixth-highest global brand valuation. For a long time, Buffett himself regularly ate at McDonald's on the way to the office. He also had family parties there. Also, he holds a Gold Card, essentially a "free McDonald's for life" in US outlets.

 Buffett bought 4.3% of McDonald's common stocks in 1996. He paid about $1.3 billion. However, he sold the shares immediately. In the 1998 annual report, Buffett admitted that it was "a very big mistake".

In March 2024, Berkshire's investment could have grown tenfold, and the total dividend received would been more than $2 billion, by just sitting tight and doing nothing.

Buffett bought McDonald's first as a food franchise. It came with a real estate business.

However, later he realized that it would be hard to separate the two due to franchise deals in 100-plus countries. He felt that people move easily to try various food options. So, customer loyalty was compromised at McDonald's, but it is not in Coca-Cola and Gillette. Also, he became sensitive to the stock price movement.

On the plus side, McDonald's brand travels the world easily. It could grow revenue with international business. Thus, the business could expand through franchises, letting it grow along with new offerings.

———

Buffett's own words [1998 AR]:

"I need to make a confession (ugh): The portfolio actions I took in 1998 actually decreased our gain for the year. In particular, my decision to sell McDonald's was a very big mistake. Overall, you would have been better off last year if I had regularly snuck off to the movies during market hours."

Lessons:

1. Few brands travel the world easily. The beauty lies in the standardized setup and

processes to create an identity in the consumer's experience.

2. These businesses are worth holding for long-term capital appreciation and dividends.

3. A successful investor acts when required and makes money from inactivity. Inactivity is understated in the investment world.

4. Involvement in the hyperactive often breeds mistakes.

Chapter 13: Buying 2% in Silver
[Year – 1996]

Unconventional 'Investment' – A Trade.

In 1996, Buffett bought 111 million ounces of silver. The purchase was close to a quarter of annual world production at the time. The total investment topped $650 million. Later, he booked a $97 million gain. It was an unusual investment or to be precise, a 'trade'.

Buffett was betting on the basic principle of economics: the supply and demand gap. He was bullish on the increased use of silver. It could be used in photography, industries, and jewellery.

Silver is produced as a by-product from mining gold, copper, zinc, and so on. So, as demand increases, supply will be tight. This raises silver prices. Buffett had been tracking silver prices and the market scenario for over 30 years. Then, he bought fast and sold faster for 2% of the total Berkshire's capital.

You can argue about his discipline and patience. On the other hand, it could have taken his mind-share and time. As a hobby... sure, have fun, but not as an intelligent investor!

———

Buffett's own words [1998 AGM, commenting on Silver trade.]:

"We think right now that — or we thought last summer when we started buying it — that the price we bought it, that that was not an equilibrium price, and that sooner or later — and we didn't think it was imminent, because we don't wait till things are imminent."

Bonus: Munger's own words [1998 AGM]:

"Well, I think this whole episode will have about as much impact on Berkshire Hathaway's future as 's bridge playing. You've got a line of activity where once every 30 or 40 years you can do something employing 2 percent of assets. This is not a big deal for Berkshire. The fact that it keeps amused and not doing counterproductive things..."

PS: *Even though Berkshire made some gains in this silver transaction episode. I think it distracts an Equity Investor. It takes their mental, capital, and time resources. Hence, I took it as a mistake. Although Munger was polite by downplaying it as a hobby.*

Lessons:

1. To succeed in commodity, a trader needs
    to know the market. This means supply-
    and-demand scenarios, and the
    discipline to wait for a chance to trade.

2. An equity investor might trade
    commodities as a hobby. They do it to
    take once-a-while advantage of changes
    in supply and demand.

Chapter 14: Costco Wholesale Corporation
[Year – 1998]

Simply Act When an Opportunity Knocks.

Costco is an American multinational corporation headquartered in the state of Washington. It operates as a chain of membership-only big-box warehouses and club retail stores, having a presence across 800 locations worldwide. Costco is one of the dominant warehouse retailers based on the value offered for its merchandise.

Buffett purchased Costco shares in 1998. He bought them in small amounts at $28 each, adjusted for a split. Costco's management invited Buffett on board, but he declined. He suggested they check with Charlie Munger. Munger accepted it and was on the board till his death in November 2023

Buffett understood the Costco business model and its competitive strength. Munger and he were vocal in admiring Costco's business during Berkshire's annual meetings. However, he never raised a stake in the company; there was no clear explanation for why.

Buffett might be worried about competition from e-commerce, but Costco proved that wrong.

Buffett sold his Costco shares in 2020 for $1.3 billion when the stock price was $350 per share. Since then stock rose to $736 per share in March of 2024.

Note: I do not like to judge solely based on the stock price movement.

The Costco business is doing well, and its moat is intact. The revenue and profit are growing y-o-y. In 2023 grew by 6% and 9%, respectively. However, I hardly believe that he did it to free up the capital to invest during the COVID-19 pandemic. Considering that the $1.3 billion stake sale won't move the needle for Berkshire Hathaway Inc.

————

Buffett's own words [2000 AGM]:

"Charlie is a director of Costco, so he's a — Costco is an absolutely fabulous organization. We should have owned a lot of Costco over the years and we — I blew it. Charlie was for it, but I blew it"

Bonus: Munger's own words [2011 AGM]:

"I really admire Costco. And that's one of the pleasures of my life, is interfacing with those people. (on board) *Costco, of course, is a — a business that became the best in the world in its category, and it did it with an extreme meritocracy and an extreme ethical duty, self-imposed, to take all its cost advantages as fast as it could accumulate them and pass them onto the customers. And, of course, that created ferocious customer loyalty."*

Lessons:

1. An investor loads up on the shares of a company within his or her circle of competence.

2. Selling a wonderful business based on price movement is not an investment (business-like). It's a trading strategy.

Chapter 15: General Reinsurance Corporation
[Year – 1998]

Equity is Priceless and Investigation is Basic in Investment.

In 1998, General Reinsurance (General Re) was the largest U.S. property-casualty reinsurer. It owned 82% of the world's oldest reinsurance company, Cologne Re. These two companies operated in 124 countries.

Buffett purchased General Re for the exchange of 272,200 Class-A shares of Berkshire Hathaway Inc. The overall acquisition was valued at $15.9 billion, based on Berkshire's closing price on 31st December 1998. The transaction had increased Berkshire's outstanding shares by a humongous 21.8%. *What a dilution!*

Based on the latest Berkshire share price, the purchase was valued at more than $175 billion and counting...

There might be a few reasons for the transaction. Buffett wanted to grow Berkshire's reinsurance portfolio. He also wanted to add more power to its cash-generating machine, called "float". Consider: 1) He had acquired GEICO two years earlier. He might have wanted to strengthen it more. (2) In the mid-1990s, Buffett was under pressure. He might have been desperate to act during the technology boom, and 3) He thought Berkshire's shares were overvalued. So, issuing shares would be a better idea.

*****

As in a typical acquisition, issues start popping up one by one later. As it is often said, you understand how deep the water is when you get into it.

By the 2009 annual meeting, Buffett confessed his mistake in acquiring General Re. The following were the issues:

1. Buffett had known the company for a long time. He was impressed by the top-notch reputation General Re enjoyed in the insurance world. But the story turned the other way around. General Re got into regulatory challenges because of past actions. Berkshire needed to fix it. The managers were replaced: this was unusual. Buffett's mantra in acquiring businesses was to ensure as passionate managers as he could not supply them. He hunts for a readily available complete package as an operating business.

2. General Re's insurance underwriting
    had many bad practices. For one, they
    did not evaluate risks well. They set
    foolish prices and terms, and they did
    not limit risk from single and unrelated
    events. Hence, it suffered hugely in the
    2001 September 11 attack on the World
    Trade Center. Buffett termed General Re
    operations as "dangerously weak" in the
    2001 Berkshire annual report.

3. Buffett underestimated General Re's
    derivative portfolio. It took years and
    much effort. New managers, Joe
    Brandon and Tad Monross had to take
    control of General Re's operations. They
    also had to unwind these derivative
    positions for a long time.

4. During General Re's purchase, they
    overstated profits. They also failed to
    account for $800 million in loss costs in
    earlier transactions, resulting in
    overpaying for the acquisition.

Later, Berkshire consolidates its reinsurance
businesses into a group. General Re is part of the
group. This insurance and reinsurance are a key
group. They fuel Berkshire's float. Early in 2024,
the float had grown to $169 billion.

______

Buffett's own words [2016 AR]:

"It was, nevertheless, a terrible mistake on my part to issue 272,200 shares of Berkshire in buying General Re, an act that increased our outstanding shares by a whopping 21.8 percent. My error caused Berkshire shareholders to give far more than they received (a practice that — despite the Biblical endorsement — is far from blessed when you are buying businesses) … After some early problems, General Re has become a fine insurance operation that we prize,"

Lessons:

1. Diluting equity should be a last resort for a "mature" and "responsible" company. An investor could consider it in the framework while deciding on an investment.

2. We need to understand a peculiar fact about equity. Once issued, it stays on a company's books unless bought back. Reversing these equity dilutions is tough and many times costly to reverse. But if the same transaction is done in cash or through debt, it could have been easily fixed by paying with operating cash.

3. In investing, I look for the company's
    equity issuance "habits". If a company
    issues ESOPs or dilutes for expansions, I
    consider them in the evaluation process.
    This is not seen as widely used.

4. Any kind of desperation to act is an
    investment mistake.

5. The investigation is vital in investment. It
    is basic to understand past events and
    their impacts on future business affairs.
    And we are investing for the future!

6. Evaluating Management is a tricky part.
    An investor needs to study past behavior.
    They also need to watch for future
    actions.

Chapter 16: PetroChina Company Ltd.

[Year – 2007]

Early Sale.

PetroChina is a Chinese oil and gas company. It is part of the state-owned China National Petroleum Corporation (CNPC). CNPC founded was founded in 1999, and PetroChina is a listing arm of it. As of today, in 2024, CNPC is Asia's largest oil and gas company.

During 2002-03, Buffett purchased PetroChina "H" shares when the market cap was just $37 billion and produced 3% of world oil. He invested $488 million in 1.3% of publicly outstanding stocks (90% owned by the Chinese government).

This was the first purchase made by Buffett in China. Buffett and Munger felt the company was worth $100 billion. They considered its global energy assets and future cash flow. It was very cheaply priced, so a clear value buy. The managers at PetroChina built valuable oil & gas reserves across the globe. The Cherry on the cake: the company planned to pay out 45% of earnings to the shareholders.

In the 2007 Berkshire AGM, a resolution was presented that called for divesting from PetroChina due to moral reasons, but it was rejected. The resolution pointed out humanitarian issues in Sudan, where the parent company was active. However, soon, Buffett sold the entire stake. He did so for a handsome gain of $4 billion.

There were multiple reasons to sell the stake in PetroChina. Buffett cited issues like the overvaluation of the company, percentage acquisition limitation as a major Chinese government-owned entity (90%), US-China relations, tax laws, and Chinese policies.

Later, Buffett proclaimed that, if PetroChina is available as a value buy, he would take it again.

After selling the stake in PetroChina, the stock price shot up. It became the world's first trillion-dollar company and the most valued. The buy-and-hold strategy was missing here. Despite initial gains, Buffett sold Berkshire's stake in PetroChina too early. He missed out on further advances in the company's prospects and value.

———

Buffett's own words [2006 AGM, responding to resolution to divest in PetroChina]:

"I don't think it's proper for us to divest our shares in PetroChina. They would be sold to somebody else. I think the proponents of the motion probably would like the idea that the price of the stock would go down. But we don't sell stocks, you know, basically to try and drive them down in price. We might sell PetroChina if it went up enough, but we would not be selling it to try and drive down the price, because all that would be doing is giving a bargain to somebody else who is buying the stock of PetroChina."

Note: *In reality, it happened exactly opposite. Buffett sold PetroChine in 2007, and the stock price went way up after that. The business expanded. Hence, I count it as a mistake.*

Bonus: Munger's own words [2004 AGM, responding to the PetroChina buy.]:

"If a thing is cheap enough, obviously you can afford a little more country risk, or regulatory risk, or whatever. This is not complicated."

Lessons:

1. Selling in the market is tricky to avoid regrets or overwhelming feelings. The

weighing on risk probabilities needs a well-defined investment framework. It helps to address both facets of opportunity to gain and probability of loss on the judgment day of the transaction.

2. As the capital base balloons, the opportunity size shrinks for an investor. It is a tough situation to manage performance and risk.

Chapter 17: Energy Future Holdings Corp.
[Year – 2007]

"Trees Don't Grow to the Sky." - German Proverb

In 2007, KKR & Co, TPG Capital, and Goldman Sachs Capital Partners which are Private Equity (PE) players acquired TXU Corp for $45 billion. TXU Corp was a Texas-based utility company. The company was the fifth largest energy concern in the US. This leveraged buy-out created Energy Future Holding Corporation (EFHC).

A typical leveraged buyout game is to buy, hold, and improve the entity's finances. Then, you exit by reselling or making the company public. The exit route is predefined during the buy.

In 2007, the deal was made with cheaply and easily available debt. As in a typical bull market, the deal was made at a higher valuation.

Buffett bought $2 billion worth of debt (bonds). He did not consult Munger. Berkshire became a major holder of Energy Future Holding's bonds. The key assumption was that natural gas prices would stay high and keep growing; it was already at a peak in 2007. These high prices would keep electricity prices high. They would also generate more revenue for the company.

The US financial market crashed in 2008. This brought down the gas prices from $7-$8 per million British thermal units to $4 in 2011. The advances in technology and higher availability of gas, using shale play, added to ease the price. Hence, the company's revenue dropped substantially. The PE players rolled over debt payments for years. They did it through refinancing and by extending repayment schedules. The overall debt payment was ballooned.

EFHC's revenue had dropped over the years, while the operational costs were increased. This, plus record interest costs, made the business unviable.

Finally, in 2014 the company filed for bankruptcy. Ultimately, Berkshire lost $873 million, pre-tax.

———

Buffett's own words [2013 AR]:

"Most of you have never heard of Energy Future Holdings. Consider yourselves lucky; I certainly wish I hadn't... About $2 billion of the debt was purchased by Berkshire, pursuant to a decision I made without consulting with

Charlie. That was a big mistake... Next time I'll call Charlie."

Lessons:

1. Global energy prices are usually tied to supply and demand. Gas prices stay high or rise unidirectional was the assumption, so the investment was a mistake. In fact it was a trade.

2. An investor needs to watch out for higher valuations in a bull market, specifically. It is even more crucial for businesses operating in commodities or/and are regulated.

1. "Invert, always invert" in decision-making against bias is best suited here to have a robust investment framework.

3. PE has different strategies for managing the portfolio and their investments. You partner with whom you trust, and believe in their investment philosophy. An investor need to understand and distinguish different investment strategies for their advantage.

Chapter 18: ConocoPhillips Company
[Year 2008]

Euphoria Sucks.

"If you want to be wrong then follow the masses." - Socrates

ConocoPhillips is a Texas-based multinational corporation. The company was established in 1875 as Continental Oil and Transportation Company (Conoco). It became independent after the dissolution of Standard Oil. Later in 2002. It merged with Phillips Petroleum Company to form ConocoPhillips and engaged in hydrocarbon exploration and production. The company owns oil and gas assets worldwide.

Buffett started purchasing ConocoPhillips stocks in 2005. By the end of 2006, Berkshire Holding was 1.1% of the company. During this time, crude oil prices ranged between $40 to $65 per barrel. The highest euphoria in oil prices started in early 2007. The prices climbed to all time high to $147 per barrel in July 2008. *To date this price is not breached!*

During this period, Buffett was carried away by the price boom. He aggressively bought ConocoPhillips shares to take the Berkshire holding to 5.7%. The total cost of investment was $7 billion. He wanted to lock into crude prices through this buy. In this excitement, he did not discuss his thesis with Charlie Munger, Berkshire's Vice Chairman. He paid a high premium to the company when crude was in an upward trajectory.

In 2008, the US financial system was crumbled. In no time, the global market was gripped in panic. This uncertainty and fear brought down the commodity markets. Crude prices crashed in a few months to $40 in Jan 2009. ConocoPhillips' stock price took a deep dive from $70 to $28 per share in no time. The value of Berkshire's 5.7% holding in ConocoPhillips dropped to $4.4 billion by the end of 2008.

Buffett admitted the mistake right away in Berkshire's 2008 annual report. He said the timing was terrible, and it cost Berkshire billions.

This was a time when a wise and patient investor could have shopped on Wall Street. They could have done so with all their capital. This mistake costs more indirectly, through an "opportunity cost" to Berkshire. I described a few of them in a separate section of the book (Part B).

———

In Buffett's own words [2008 AR]:

"I made a major mistake of commission (and maybe more; this one sticks out). Without urging from Charlie or anyone else, I bought a large amount of ConocoPhillips stock when oil and gas prices were near their peak. I in no way anticipated the dramatic fall in energy prices that occurred in the last half of the year. I still believe the odds are good that oil sells far higher in the future than the current $40-$50 price. But so far I have been dead wrong. Even if prices should rise, moreover, the terrible timing of my purchase has cost Berkshire several billion dollars."

"When investing, pessimism is your friend, euphoria the enemy,"

Lessons:

1. Investing in oil and gas requires understanding their cycles. Many things affect prices, including cycles in regional and global economies. Also, consider geopolitical events and transportation scenarios.

2. Nothing new: don't try to time the market!

3. As always, an investor needs to watch out for euphoria within, and then outside on Wall Street. Act only when needed to your advantage.

4. 'Invert, always invert.' It is your thesis to get better insights.

5. 'Opportunity cost' is one of the basic matrices used in allocating capital. In the 2008 market crash, capital could be used well for beaten-down, attractive stocks.

Chapter 19: TESCO Plc.

[Year – 2013]

Selling is Tricky.

TESCO is a leading U.K.-based food retailer that runs a global retailing and grocery business in many countries. However, many international operations were later closed.

Buffett acquired a 2.9% stake in TESCO 2006 for $1.3 billion. Since then, he kept adding shares until 2012 to take total investment to $2.3 billion.

Buffett was impressed by TESCO's recent global expansion ambition and growth prospects. He admired the CEO, Terry Leahy's capability to execute and his overall management of a competitive retailing business. During the same time in 2006, TESCO entered the US market.

By 2013, many issues started surfacing in TESCO's operations: the company's revenue suffered and the margins contracted. At the same time, malpractices in accounting were detected.

The company overstated the accounts by £246 million. The company recognized income from suppliers improperly. They did so by "pulling it forward", but it landed them in legal trouble. TESCO group's underline reported profit before tax fell by 14.5% in 2013 and further by 6.9% in 2014. The stalwart TESCO CEO, Terry Leahy, was already retired in 2010 after a fourteen-year stint.

Buffett saw the challenges at TESCO. He sold some shares early in 2013 for a gain of $43 million. However, he delayed further sales. By then the stock price tumbled. The negative news was popping up one by one for the company. The company's US operations filed for Chapter 11 bankruptcy in mid-2013 and it later sold out to a private PE firm.

Buffett had exited completely by the end of the year. The delay and slow action caused Berkshire a total after-tax loss of $444 million. Buffett confessed to the mistake in the 2014 annual letter.

———

Buffett's in own words [2014 AR, in the context of TESCO]:

"My leisurely pace in making sales would prove expensive. Charlie calls this sort of behavior "thumb-sucking."

Lessons:

1. Selling in the market is tricky; it demands emotional stability. It pays to be philosophical about selling to avoid regret if prices rise.

2. A wise investor is disciplined. She or he does things their way, based on a framework and process. They act immediately in a controlled way when the original buy thesis fails. *I may write more about selling one day.*

3. For a retailer to expand, many things must fall in place. These include cheap procurement, efficient distribution, wide sales pricing strategies, and grow loyal customers. It gets complicated because of local and global market dynamics and competition. The competition is among local stores, discount stores, and mega-retailers. It is a tough business.

4. We need to recheck the thesis with any changes in key management as it might lead to changes in business models and the company culture.

Chapter 20: NetJets Inc.
[Year – 2009]

Costly Romantic Affair.

NetJets Inc. is an Ohio-based company that sells fractional ownership shares in private jets and runs the fleets for their owners. The company was founded in 1964 as Executive Jet Airways (EJA). Later, it changed its name to NetJets. Richard Santulli was the CEO who created the world's first fractional ownership business segment in 1986.

NetJets makes most of its money by selling part ownership of many jets. They also make money from monthly management fees, and fees for hours flown.

In 1998, Buffett purchased NetJet for a total of $725 million. The deal was to pay half in cash and the remaining by Berkshire stocks. At that time, the company was the largest private operator in the US. It had over 1,000 customers and 163 aircraft.

Buffett's acquisition rationale was: the business has top-notch service. It was present across the country and had the best safety record. This gave the company an edge and allowed them serve to customers on short notice, which other

competitors could not do. Berkshire also owned
FlightSafety, which was training NetJet pilots.

Buffett and Munger were both NetJet customers.
Buffett hoped for modest profit from NetJet
operations. Hum.. too much optimism.

NetJets's revenue had been increasing for a
couple of years. However, later in 2001, the
attack on the World Trade Center hurt the
business. The US economy also got worse, and in
2002, revenue reached record levels. However,
profits were negative because of the increase in
aircraft and operating costs. Furthermore, in
2003, the company reported a loss of $43
million due to European operations, while the
total number of customers rose nearly to 5,000.

Finally, in 2005, in Berkshire's annual report,
Buffett admitted that he was "dead wrong" when
he expected NetJet to earn money for Berkshire.
The revenue was increasing and so was
expenditure, at a faster pace. The company
incurred a $80 million pre-tax loss mainly
because of unfavourable contracts with
customers to meet demand from costly sub-
contracting to charter services. It was not able to
recover the cost. Furthermore, NetJet
expenditure had increased for the addition of
newer planes to meet the demand. A typical case
of higher cost for expansion of business.

The biggest mistake at NetJets was buying planes at fictitiously high prices compared to the prices at which they were sold later to customers for fractional ownership. In AR 2008, NetJets incurred charges of $54 million to write down the aircraft fleet. Richard Santulli resigned as CEO and in 2009, Dave Sokol became the new CEO. He started to optimize the operations and cost of NetJet. The 2009 AGM discussion suggests that a "manager-related issue" might have motivated the change.

The US economic meltdown in 2008 hurt NetJets; it dropped the demand for services. Since Berkshire's acquisition, the total loss was $157 million in 2009, while the debt rose from $102 million to $1.4 billion. It was due to the commitment to purchase a total of 556 aircraft by 2015.

NetJet could have gone bankrupt, but Berkshire's strength kept it running. Since then, it continued efforts to sustain the business by optimizing operational costs. It tried to get into Saudi Arabia and the Chinese market, with no success. It began introducing new plans and cards to flyers.

Again, the company took a hit at the beginning of the 2020 pandemic. NetJet remains a dominant player in its space nonetheless. But there hasn't been much discussion of how profitable it is for its Berkshire owners. It is wrapped under the service business segment of Berkshire.

———

Buffett's own words [2009 AR]:

"Without Berkshire's guarantee of this debt, NetJets would have been out of business. It's clear that I failed you in letting NetJets descend into this condition. But, luckily, I have been bailed out. Maintaining top-of-the-line standards is the right thing to do, but I also have a selfish reason for championing this policy. My family and I have flown more than 5,000 hours on NetJets."

Bonus: Munger's own words [2010 AGM, while addressing to a query related to NetJets's problems.]:

"If we buy 30 big businesses and generally let the people who run them successfully and before run them with very little interference from headquarters, and it works out 95 percent of the time very well, and we have one episode (referred to NetJet) when the basic franchise was protected but we lost profit opportunities for a while, it's not a big failure record."

Lessons:

1. Some businesses suck in too much capital to expand. It demands external capital, either using debt or equity. As they are unable to produce sufficient retained earnings.

2. Investors need to watch out for real owner's earnings over longer periods. Few traders take advantage of expansion announcements. However, this strategy might work for a short duration with its limitations.

3. Not all subscription businesses that collect advance money from customers will succeed. The underlines business economics take precedence.

4. Having the right management is crucial. They must have an ownership mind-set. This is key for equity investors.

Chapter 21: International Business Machine Corp. (IBM)

[Year – 2011]

Honor Own Circle of Competence.

IBM is an over-century-old technology company. It was the front-runner for many technological firsts and innovations. However, since the 1990s, companies have been struggling and downsizing operations often.

Buffett had been studying IBM for over 50 years before he first purchased it in 2011. He acquired a total of 5.5% outstanding shares for $10.9 billion. This took IBM investment to the top four of Berkshire along with American Express, Coca-Cola, and Wells Fargo.

Buffett bet on four things: 1) IBM's share buybacks, 2) dividends, 3) management, and 4) customer "stickiness" from large deals.

He was fascinated by IBM's investments. He used almost one page of Berkshire's 2011 annual report to explain IBM's repurchase policy. He was very bullish on repurchases. He speculated that IBM could buy back all the shares someday. That would leave only Berkshire's holding of 63.9 million shares (*from 5.5% to 100%*

holding!). He also committed to giving Berkshire employees one day of paid leave, if it happens.

Buffett was confident about IBM's business outlook; but he acknowledged that it was not as "bullet-proof" as Coca-Cola. He kept on purchasing IBM shares till 2015 to take his holding to 8.4%, for a total investment of $13.8 billion.

However, since 2014, IBM's stock price has been dropping. It has been accused of financial engineering its accounts. Berkshire's holding value dropped by 19% to $11.1 billion. During an AGM, a shareholder questioned the logic of holding IBM. In response, both Buffett and Munger endorsed IBM as having been purchased at a reasonable price.

There were fundamental business issues with IBM; it was falling behind other technology competitors in products like Cloud-based and in-service contracts. Later in 2017, Buffett admitted his mistake. He was still thinking of IBM as a big, strong company. However, he acknowledged that IBM has bigger and stronger competitors.

He was able to sell a reasonable quantity of shares above $180 per share versus the original cost of $170. Finally, by the end of 2018, he sold his complete stake in IBM.

Buffett's IBM purchase was one of the biggest mistakes. He had crossed his '*Circle of Competence*'.

The mistake was further compounded by holding onto the loser even though it was clear that the company was struggling. The advances in technology and fast pace of competitors, like Amazon Cloud (AWS), disrupted the market.

———

Buffett's own words: [2012 AGM]:

"Well, I would say that I do not understand the moat around an IBM as well as I understand the moat around a Coca-Cola. But I feel good enough about IBM that we've put a considerable amount of money in it."   "The chances of being way wrong in IBM are probably less, at least for us, than being way wrong with Google or Apple. But that doesn't mean that those — the latter two companies — aren't going to do, say, far better than IBM."

[2013 AGM]: *"I've got enough conviction about IBM's position that we took a very large position."*

[2017 AGM] *"I made a large investment in IBM, and — which has not turned out that well. We haven't lost money. But in terms of the bull market we've been in, it's been a significant laggard."*

Bonus: Munger's own words: [2017 AGM]:

"Well, we avoided the tech stocks, because we felt we had no advantage there and other people did. And I think that's a good idea not to play where the other people are better."

Lessons:

1. A disciplined investor stays in their own circle of competence. She or he understands its boundaries and honors them.

2. The key criteria for an investment is the business's long-term competitive edge so it can deliver satisfactory returns to the owners.

3. It is a **BIG** challenge for investors in an ever-changing technological world. Investing is becoming more complex as more and more brain power is getting dedicated to it.

4. Share repurchases and dividends are important in an investment theme; however, business performance needs to lead them.

PS: *Buffett has always been shy away from technology. However, I still wonder why he decided to invest in IBM, and not in any other technology companies.*

Chapter 22: Lubrizol Corporation
[Year – 2011]

Reputation, the Currency of Trust

Lubrizol makes specialty chemicals and additives that serve many industries worldwide. These include markets for transport, drugs, industries, and consumers.

Buffett acquired all outstanding shares of Lubrizol in March 2011 for $8.7 billion. Lubrizol merged with Berkshire later in September 2011.

A senior executive at Berkshire who ran subsidiaries like MidAmerica, NetJets, and other small subsidiaries. He joined Berkshire when it acquired MidAmerica in 1999. Since then Buffett had high regard for him and proclaimed him as a big asset to Berkshire. He considered Buffett as a friend and mentor. Over the years, he was rumored as Buffett's successor.

He introduced the Lubrizol company to Buffett in early 2011. Buffett agreed to the acquisition, as he trusted the senior executive. The deal happened in no time, but there was a catch.

Before introducing the company to Buffett, the senior executive privately bought shares in Lubrizol, against the corporate governance rule.

He did not disclose his purchase to Buffett.
When Berkshire announced the acquisition,
Lubrizol's stock prices rose. The senior executive
sold the shares and made a profit of $3 million.

Soon after that, the senior executive's private
transaction was exposed. He resigned. He had
violated insider trading rules. The irrational
behavior sucks an intelligent person too. For
someone who had earned $24 million as
compensation in the previous year, 2010 was
unimaginable. He lost his reputation and his
candidacy as the future Berkshire CEO.

This is a case study for *"Why leaders lose their
way?"* Buffett had over-trusted the senior
executive. He should have dug deeper to
understand the past transactions and details.

In 2012 at Berkshire's annual meeting, Buffett
said it was a "big mistake" not to quiz him.

*****

Lubrizol's business front:

Lubrizol's specialty chemical business operates
in a global market, known to be competitive.
Many of the products are hazardous materials.
The outside factors govern the business,
including federal and state laws. There are laws
to protect the environment and foreign laws

about where it operates. It is a damn complex business where anything could go wrong.

In 2014, Lubrizol acquired the oilfield chemicals and drilling fluids business of Weatherford International Plc for $750 million and formed a new entity: Oilfield Solutions.

This was a costly affair. It later shut down many of the oilfield solution locations. Also, most of the employees were terminated and the unit was closed down, while some parts were integrated with other businesses. The pre-tax loss reported was $365 million.

Later in the 2015 annual meeting, Buffett said Lubrizol's purchase was a "big mistake."

———

Buffett's own words [2011 AGM. Described the sequence of events in this episode and Lubrizol affair.]:

"He (the senior executive) said, "Well, take a look at it. It — you know, it might fit Berkshire."

And I said, "How come?" And he said, well — he said, "I've owned it and it's a good company. It's a Berkshire-type company."

And, you know, I obviously made a big mistake by not saying, "Well, when did you buy it?"

But I think if somebody says I've owned the stock, you know it sounds to me like they didn't buy it the previous week.

So there we are with a situation, which is sad for Berkshire, sad for (him), still inexplicable in my mind, and we will undoubtedly get more questions on that. We'll be glad to answer them."

Bonus: Munger's own words [2011 AGM in the context of this episode and Lubrizol affair.]:

"Well, I think it's generally a mistake to assume that rationality is going to be perfect, even in very able people. We prove that pretty well, regularly."

Lessons:

1. An investor needs to have insight into the nature of the business and its economic character. A chemical business is competitive and governed by many environmental laws. Plus, it is exposed to innovations and market disruptions.

2. Insight into management behavior is challenging. As investors, we need to deal

with it.

3. One way is to look at how management has behaved in the past. Are there any red flags in the operation of the business? Also, it was vital to understand the treatment given to the shareholders.

   One easy trick that, I use is the nature of the business they operate. The businesses that test a management's ethics at every step are challenging. It is easy to fall prey to irrational behavior. Though, it is not a 'bullet-proof' strategy.

Chapter 23: The Kraft Heinz Company
[Year – 2015]

Overpaid for Limited Brand Power

H. J. Heinz was a global food products producer and marketer. Its products are in many categories and owns many brands. They range from ketchup, cheese, sauces, and meals to soups, snacks, and infant nutrition.

In 2013, Buffett invested $12.25 billion in Heinz Holding. Heinz Holding then bought H. J. Heinz Company in June of 2013. Berkshire holds 50% of Heinz Holding, using common stocks, stock warrants, and preferred stock. The preferred stock is entitled to a 9% annual dividend. After three years, it had a callable option at the appropriate value.

In an unusual acquisition, Buffett partnered with 3G Capital Inc., a private equity firm. 3G invested the remaining 50% in Heinz Holding. They received common stocks with equal voting rights. So, both parties invested about $23.25 billion in total in a private-equity transaction. Buffett wanted this deal to be a template for similar ones in the future.

*****

Kraft Foods Group Inc. is one of the largest consumer packaged food and beverages companies in North America. It owns numerous popular brands.

In 2015, Heinz Holding acquired a majority stake in Kraft and merged as Kraft Heinz. Berkshire received a 26.6% stake in the merged entity: Kraft Heinz. Berkshire was part of the controlling group along with 3G. Kraft's acquisition cost Berkshire $9.8 billion and the merged entity $9.8 billion.

On Berkshire's books, this investment follows the "*equity*" method. As Berkshire is part of the controlling group – Heinz Holding – along with 3G.

Since its acquisition, Kraft Heinz's revenue has been struggling to grow. The company's valuation at Nasdaq reflects this, even though the company has tried to transform itself continuously through restructuring its operations. In the process, it sold off units like nuts and specialty cheese, while acquiring sauces and condiment companies.

The crux of the issue: Kraft Heinz products have limited brand power. Hence, the company faces challenges while dealing with retailers, specifically, biggies. It limits the bargaining power. While these retailers always try to push their own private brands.

One such case is Costco's 'Kirkland', marketed as better quality at a lower price. This single brand at Costco earns more than 50% of sales as compared to the overall sales of Kraft Heinz. The Kirkland brand has been around for only thirty years, while the Kraft brand has existed for more than 100 years. Also, Kraft spends heavily on advertising.

Costco tried to drop powerful brands like Coca-Cola from its shelves. But its brand power made Costco bring them back.

In 2019, Buffett admitted that he had overpaid for Kraft, although he praised the brands under the umbrella of the company.

———

Buffett's own words: [In an interview]:

"We at Kraft, Board try to push retailers hard with thought that we are stronger. We have weaker bargaining power."

[2019 AGM]: "Kraft Heinz is still doing very well, operationally. But we paid too much. If we paid 50 billion, you know, it would've been a different business. It'd still be earning the same amount. You can turn any investment into a bad deal by paying too much. What you can't do is turn any investment into a good deal by paying little, which is sort of how I started out in this world."

Bonus: Munger's own words [2019 AGM]:

"Well, it's not a tragedy that, out of two transactions, one worked wonderfully (Heinz), and the other (Kraft) didn't work so well. That happens."

Lessons:

1. The food and beverages market is becoming more competitive; as big retailers are pushing their private brands.

2. Real brand power commands a top price. It dictates pricing to distributors and retailers. Of course, the customer's pull is strong.

3. Even power brand images drift over time and ease bargaining power. Investors need to consider more challenges for these companies. E-commerce is rising, and goods move faster. Meanwhile, valuing them became a regular exercise.

4. For investors, overpaying causes two issues: a) upward potential gets limited and b) opportunity cost.

Chapter 24: Precision Castparts Corp. (PCC)

[Year – 2016]

Valuation is the Key.

PCC is a global manufacturer of complex metal parts and products. It makes castings, forgings, fasteners, and seamless pipes. These products serve the aerospace, power, energy, and other industries.

Buffett purchased PCC's shares in 2016 for about $32.7 billion. It includes $16 billion as goodwill. The whole deal was in cash.

Buffett bought PCC because it was a top supplier in its markets. PCC has long customer relationships. They have technical skills, modern facilities, and dedicated employees. This could lead to PCC maintaining a competitive advantage.

He was right in the identification of business value; however, he paid a high price. Since 2017, PCC's revenue and profits swung, based on the performance of the markets where it operates.

In 2020, during the COVID-19 pandemic, PCC suffered as it is heavily dependent on the aerospace industry. During this time, revenue dropped from $7.3 billion to $3 billion, while pre-tax earnings dropped by 64% to $650 million. Of note, PCC cut down the worldwide workforce by 40%.

Berkshire wrote down the value of PCC by $10 billion. Buffett admitted in the 2020 annual report that he had paid too much for PCC. He had been too optimistic about PCC's business potential and misjudged future earnings. In short, he miscalculated the proper price to pay for the business.

———

Buffett's own words [2020 AR]:

"Anytime we look at buying a business, we're evaluating the competitive strengths of the business, the price we have to pay, the management we got, everything. We didn't make a mistake on the management, but in terms of the earning power on average… I believe I was right in concluding that PCC would, over time, earn good returns on the net tangible assets deployed in its operations. I was wrong, however, in judging the average amount of future earnings and, consequently, wrong in my calculation of the proper price to pay for the business. PCC is far from my first error of that sort. But it's a big one."

Lessons:

1. Valuation is the key that decides the investor's gain over time. *"Price what you pay; value what you get."*

2. The casting and forging industry is competitive. Customers prefer a couple of suppliers and play around for better deals.

3. These companies get squeezed among customers, raw material suppliers, and labor. Everyone wants to take a larger share of the profit.

Chapter 25: Newspapers (Print Media)

[Years – 1969 To 2011]

No Permanence, Sold Out.

Buffett's love for the newspaper business is well known. The love goes back to his childhood when he was delivering them door-to-door, and started his entrepreneurial journey.

The first purchase he made was way back in 1969. It was Sun Newspaper Inc., a group of weekly publications in metropolitan Omaha. It was an insignificant financial transaction though. Later in 1973, he bought a 9% stake in the Washington Post Company. He got it for $9.7 million, a throwaway price.

In 1977, Buffett purchased the Buffalo News for $36 million. He kept buying newspaper businesses with daily and/or weekly circulations. Before the Internet, newspapers, TV, and magazines were the main sources of information. They covered wide topics like politics, entertainment, and sports. Print newspapers were easily available. The popular newspapers used to offer a lot of news and advertisements.

There were a few prominent reasons for Buffett's love for newspapers:

1. A leading regional paper is like a monopoly; it has pricing power and can easily raise subscription fees.
2. They can demand higher prices from advertisers
3. They generate some "float" (like insurance). They get it by receiving money from subscribers in advance.
4. They lead regional opinion and activities. They are a powerhouse.
5. It is a sticky business. A reader prefers to read the same newspaper – hook to type of articles and sections.
6. Few such companies own a lot of property like real estate, radio, and TV stations.
7. They pay dividends.

A newspaper business earns mostly from advertising apart from circulation fees. A leading newspaper typically attracts more advertisements than a small one. The main cost for a newspaper is people. Other costs include paper production and distribution. From the stock market perspective, typically newspaper/media companies have been unpopular and offer a good bargain.

These were the major reasons behind Buffett's purchases of newspaper businesses. He bought many papers to name a few: the Washington Post, the Buffalo News, the Omaha World-

Herald, News, and so forth. These have daily circulations and/or a Sunday paper.

*****

The Internet era started in the mid-1980s. Since then, print newspaper circulation has declined for clear reasons like ease of access, faster flow of information/news, wider choices to consume, no effort needed to move to read, and so forth.

In the 2006 Berkshire annual report, Buffett stated that the newspaper industry had eroded its basics. He said profits would decline. The same was proclaimed in the 2009 annual general meeting as "unending losses".

However, in 2011 Buffett contradicted his own opinion. He acquired the Omaha World-Herald Company, a publisher of daily and weekly newspapers in Nebraska and Iowa. He continued to buy more newspapers buy till 2012. He acquired a total of 28 daily newspapers for $344 million.

He bet on the local "significance" of the newspaper business and expected to get a decent return over time. He also saw some tax advantages. And of course, there was his long-term love of newspapers. He grouped media service businesses as the Buffalo News and Berkshire Hathaway (BH) Media Group. BH publishes The Omaha World-Herald and twenty-nine daily newspapers.

In 2014, Buffett sold a 28% stake in the Washington Post Company. The company was one of his favourite "permanent" holdings (as per AR 1985). This negotiated deal was for $1.1 billion with Graham Holdings, although a year back Graham's family sold it to Amazon.com's founder, Jeffrey P. Bezos.

Both Buffett and Munger knew that the print newspaper business was in a downhill slide. Circulations were dropping year-on-year along with advertisement revenues. Finally, in 2020 Buffett divorced his print media companies. He sold the Buffalo and BH Media Group. By then, the BH Group was holding a total of 31 daily and 43 weekly newspapers.

The sale was for $140 million cash to Lee Enterprises. For the successful execution of the deal, Berkshire extended a financing loan of $579 million with a hefty 9% interest rate. Berkshire might make some money on the interest over the investment time period.

———

Buffett's own words [2006 AR]:

"And fundamentals are definitely eroding in the newspaper industry, a trend that has caused the profits of our Buffalo News to decline. The skid will almost certainly continue... Now, however, almost all newspaper owners realize

that they are constantly losing ground in the battle for eyeballs. Simply put, if cable and satellite broadcasting, as well as the internet, had come along first, newspapers as we know them probably would never have existed... We hope that some combination of print and online will ward off economic doomsday for newspapers, and we will work hard in Buffalo to develop a sustainable business model. I think we will be successful. But the days of lush profits from our newspaper are over."

Lessons:

1. An investor should never say "never". There is nothing like permanence in business and in life.

2. An investor needs to be agile to act quickly when the original story breaks down, rather than be carried away by denial bias.

3. Generally, doing a transaction purely for tax advantages might be a mistake.

Chapter 26: Manufacturing, Service, and Retailing Operations
[Year - 2015]

Capital Allocation is Vita.

Buffett has been acquiring companies in manufacturing, service, and retail for years. He grouped these businesses as "Manufacturing, Service, and Retailing" in Berkshire Hathaway Inc.'s annual report.

However, in the 2015 annual report, he confessed that he had made a mistake. He put too much capital into this segment.

The businesses in the group sell products from lollipops to jet airplanes. Few businesses are exceptional. They have great economics, however, earning profits of 25% to over 100% after tax, while other stocks generate returns in the range of 12% to 20%.

One such case is McLane Company, a wholesale distributor across the US. This B2B business serves customers like Walmart, 7-Eleven, and Yum! brands and others. The business model demands high-volume sales, rapid inventory turnover, and stringent cost controls.

The big mistake was allocating capital as it led to poor returns for Berkshire owners because of the high premium paid for these businesses. In the 2015 annual report, this segment reported total assets of $78.5 billion. This total includes $30.3 billion of goodwill and "other intangible assets". They earn decent pre-tax returns, but these returns seem mediocre compared to the acquisition cost.

In recent times, Berkshire took a loss on goodwill impairment on the balance sheet. In the 2023 AR, for manufacturing, service, and retail operations, the total assets were $191.6 billion. Goodwill and other intangible assets reached $34.3 billion.

I believe the goodwill and intangible numbers are high for Berkshire because it buys operating businesses. It is at the core of Berkshire's acquisition principle. If it had bought troubled businesses 'distressed sales', the story would have been different altogether for Berkshire.

———

Buffett's own words [2015 AR, while reporting the business segment]:

"In most of these cases, I was wrong in my evaluation of the economic dynamics of the company or the industry in which it operates, and we are now paying the price for my mis-

judgments. At other times, I stumbled in evaluating either the fidelity or the ability of incumbent managers or ones I later appointed."

Lessons:

1. The acquisitions with goodwill and other intangible assets make sense when they bring more cash-generating power to the company.

2. An investor needs to scrutinize these acquisitions given the benefits to the owner for the premium paid. Furthermore, watch out for the treatment given to them and the possibility of a write-off in the future.

Chapter 27: Taiwan Semiconductor Manufacturing Company Ltd. (TSMC)
[Year 2023]

Risk Management and Capital Allocation are the Core of Investing.

TSMC is a highly valuable company in the world in semiconductor contract manufacturing and design. The company has a total of thirteen fabs operating; eleven are concentrated in Taiwan and one each in the US and China. The new fab facilities in the US and Japan are under construction, and one more is planned in Germany.

Most global fabless semiconductor companies use TSMC's fab services. In 2023, the company's revenue was $71.3 billion, and net income reached to $27.7 billion. In Q3 CY2022, Buffett bought sixty million shares worth $4.1 billion. This made Berkshire one of the largest TSMC shareholders.

The reason for buying was that TSMC is one of the best-run and most important companies in the world. The importance of chip manufacturing was felt from 2021-22 when the world was facing a shortage. In short, they are critical in a world where technology usage growing exponentially. Buffett predicted that the dominance of TSMC would be there for years ahead.

So far so good. However, within a few months, in Q1 CY2023, Buffett sold almost all his stake in TSMC. This was against his buy-and-hold strategy. Meanwhile, there was no change in the company's business and chip market scenario. In fact, earnings could be higher in the future because of expansions and demand growth.

During the 2023 Berkshire AGM, Buffett clarified that the only reason for the TSCM sale was that he had re-evaluated "certain things" in the region. It sounds more like a geo-political issue. There was no change in the facts on the ground for the company when Buffett bought and sold his shares.

TSMC has been proven to be a great business and meets Berkshire's investment criteria well. Although Buffett wanted to give it a miss.

In my view, Buffett missed a critical point: TSMC is a major player globally. It serves leading fabless companies across the globe, including Apple, AMD, ARM, Broadcom, Nvidia, Marvell, Qualcomm, and others. If anything happens to TSMC due to geopolitics, these companies will suffer too. As you know, building a fab facility takes technology, resources, and time.

In early 2024, this story is still playing out. Let's revisit it, sometime more to write in the future.

———

Buffett's own words [2023 AGM]:

"While I wish we hadn't sold Taiwan Semiconductor, I've reevaluated my position in light of certain events that were going on."

Bonus: Munger's own words [2023 AGM]:

"Well, my view is that should feel comfortable if he (Buffett) wants to." (After selling TSMC. Munger sounded more gentle. And it sounds more as a mistake. But *comfort* has taken over in this case.)

Lessons:

1. Having a business in a single region or distributed across the globe brings its own challenges. The concentration of risk comes with efficiency and less overhead costs. While having operations spread across many locations brings other sets

of challenges. The company needs to open a new facility and maintain it. Plus, it will need to follow different regional laws and cultures. It must also deal with currency fluctuations, logistics, and the availability of skilled labor and administrative resources.

2. If an investor finds a wonderful business with a long-term competitive advantage, operated by able and trusted people and available at a price that you like, then it is time to seize the opportunity.

3. Future events are uncertain, and an investor needs to take a judgmental view. Given the risks and rewards, the investor always needs to factor in capital allocation.

In my view, this kind of unique and wonderful business might need special investment treatment. In light of known risk factors, she or he might allocate a small fraction of their capital to join the journey. So, capital allocation is critical for long-term investment success.

<u>PART – B</u>: Failed to Capitalize in 2008 Crash

In 2008, the US economy was in turmoil, post the Lehman Brothers failure. This event dragged the whole world into a financial crisis. The *trust* in transactions dropped to the lowest level. The worst effect was seen in the US economy and local businesses.

In 2008, Berkshire reported its worst performance since Buffett took over in 1965. Berkshire's net worth dropped by $11.8 billion while book value per share lowered by 9.6%. This was the second drop. The first was in 2001 by 6.2%.

Most of Berkshire's businesses suffered from losses or business contraction. Marketable securities — stocks and bonds — dropped in value. As you know, this is a typical phenomenon in a bear market, where blood is in the streets.

An experienced and patient investor could recognize the opportunity to seize it. Might be a lifetime opportunity to go shopping. Also, this is the time when an investor needs to be extra diligent. *A dollar is more worth than usual!* So, discipline is a must in allocating capital and buying businesses available at throwaway prices. Peculiar mistakes are 'extra' costly.

The following is a list of mistakes made by Buffett during this time:

2. Buffett was busy making fixed-income deals with preferred share options: General Electric, Goldman Sachs, and Wrigley.

3. He sold shares in companies that he had held for a long time, despite being good business: J&J, P&G.

4. He adventured into foreign bank investments and lost: Irish banks

5. Buy high and sell low error: ConocoPhillips

6. Derivative transactions

Buffett bought a total of $14.5 billion in fixed-income securities in Wrigley, Goldman Sachs, and General Electric. This financing had preferential treatment: a fixed coupon for the initial period with an option to convert to common stock. Ideally, this was the time to buy a depressed common stock. The opportunity cost was at its peak!

Secondly, Buffett sold some long holdings like in Johnson & Johnson, and Procter & Gamble. The reasoning was to maintain some level of 'float', but at what cost?

As discussed in an earlier chapter, Buffett bought ConocoPhillips during the oil boom and sold company shares during the 2008 market crash. The cost of purchase was $7 billion, and he sold when the market valued them at $4.4 billion.

In the following chapters, we glance at them and learn from the mistakes.

Note: *Though Buffett might have left some money on the table in 2008, his purpose might have been to support the US financial system and bring back the confidence. However, I included this section for investors to learn the importance of capital allocation and to make rational decisions.*

Chapter 28: General Electric Corporation (GE)

[Year – 2008]

Opportunity Cost.

GE is a century-old company. Thomas Edison, an innovator and businessman, along with JP Morgan and Charles Coffin, founded it in 1892. It was an innovative company that made many products like electric bulbs, X-ray machines, washing machines, and a variety of consumer products. The company operates in many industries like aerospace, power, digital, additive manufacturing, and finance.

Under the leadership of Jack Welch, the company thrived in the '80s and '90s. GE became a diverse conglomerate and reached second on the list of most valuable US companies.

The major fault line appeared when GE Capital the financing arm started leveraged buyout deals. It accumulated a huge $650 billion in so-called assets. It also got $550 billion in debt by 2007. The arm was adding almost 50% of profits to the parent company. *The rating agencies assigned AAA to GE!*

Of note, the 2008 market crash was catastrophic for GE. It became more like a financial company, rather than an innovation-driven manufacturing entity. The sustainability of GE became questionable. As GE Capital was not a bank, the US Federal Reserve could not help it. GE's meltdown could have been catastrophic for the US economy, which was already in limbo.

Buffett agreed to finance GE to survive. He bought $3 billion of preferred stock with a 10% annual dividend. The deal offered the option to convert to common stocks at a fixed price in the next five years. It helped GE to survive. Buffett had displayed his token of confidence in the company.

In 2017, Buffett sold all GE shares. Berkshire enjoyed a $1.5 billion (50%) return on the deal. GE is a struggling business now, trying to survive in a fast-paced arena of technological innovations. Furthermore, GE stock has been struggling to perform till 2022. Note: *I don't like to talk about stock prices as an indicator here. The "efficient-market hypothesis" has its limitations.*

Buffett might have helped GE to survive, but he did not gain the return he sought for Berkshire. It might have been the emotional appeal of extending help that made him structure a sub-dude deal. He could have structured a better deal to get a bigger slice of the company and its assets for Berkshire. It could have been given more dividends since GE is a consistent dividend-paying company.

______

Buffett's own words [2009 AGM]:

"I felt good about those companies, in terms of the quality of the businesses they had and the quality of the management. But it was the terms, primarily, that caused us to make those deals."

"You mentioned Goldman Sachs, and we also did with General Electric, in September or early October of 2008. We probably could actually have extracted better terms. You know, I think it might have been counterproductive in the end, but I was - we would have done better, incidentally, financially, if we'd really waited until the panic developed further - because I didn't know how far it would develop - but we could have made a lot better purchases three or four or five months later than we did at that time."

Lessons:

1. Whenever you hear management talking about diversification, you need to become alert.

*I ran away from financial
companies that talked about
'innovation in finances and
products'.*

2. As an investor, you need to decide
    when, where, and how much money
    to leave on the table.

Chapter 29: The Goldman Sachs Group Inc.
[Year – 2008]

Relations and Power Matters'.

Goldman Sachs is a leading investment banking firm. The company is known for providing consulting services globally; it also does wealth management, mutual funds, and related operations.

In the 2008 market crash, Goldman's value dropped sharply. It was struggling to execute its operations, so Buffett put $5 billion into Goldman. The deal was structured as follows:

1. Term: Berkshire received "perpetual" preferred shares carrying a 10% annual dividend.

    Outcome: Goldman 2011 bought them back by paying a total of $640 million and a total dividend of $1.1 billion. It was a 35% gain in two and half years.

2. Term: 43.5 million worth of warrants priced at $115 per share to execute before Oct 1, 2013.

    Outcome: In 2009, the Goldman share price fell to $50-$55 per share. In 2013, after conversion, Berkshire got about a

3% stake in Goldman. During conversion, the prevailing market price was around $125 per share (+$10 gains per share in four years). Buffett later sold the complete holding for $2.3 billion in 2020 during the COVID-19 pandemic.

Buffett knew Goldman executives; they had helped him in many ways in previous decades. He might have done the deal to help them.

———

Buffett's comments on the deal are mentioned in the GE story.

Lessons:

1. Understandably, businesses are done with personal relationships. However, as an investor, watch out for the intent behind the transactions.

2. In a depressed stock market, getting into a fixed-price deal is most likely a bad idea.

Chapter 30: Wrigley Company
[Year – 2008]

Costly Financing.

Wrigley was founded back in 1891. It is in the simple business of making and selling candy and chewing gum. It is a well-known brand and sells products worldwide.

In mid-2008, Mars Inc. a family-owned global giant in candy, drinks, food, and pet foods wanted to buy Wrigley for $23 billion. This would make it the world's biggest gum maker.

Buffett understood the business. He was ready to finance the deal along with Goldman Sachs and JPMorgan. Berkshire financed a total of $6.5 billion. The deal was a mix of preferred stocks and debt. It was structured as follows:

1. Term: A subscription to the preferred stock worth $2.1 billion. It came with a 10% stake in Wrigley and a 5% annual dividend.

    Outcome: Buffett exited in 2016 with a $2.5 billion gain. It got about $840 million in dividends over the eight-year holding period.

2. Term: Received $4.4 billion worth
    Wrigley bonds carrying 11.45% interest
    rate and maturity in 2018.

    Outcome: Mars repurchased the debt
    early in 2013. Berkshire received about
    $5.1 billion. This includes an extra $680
    million for premature withdrawal (called
    in). It also includes $2.5 billion in
    interest over five years.

Buffett almost doubled his money in the whole
transaction. The deal looks decent on an average
day in the market. However, making big debt
investments during a stock market crash doesn't
go with the saying, *"Be fearful when others are
greedy. Be greedy when others are fearful.""*

Nonetheless, the story turned into a "mistake".
To do these finances, Buffett sold shares of
companies like J&J and P&G during the 2008
market crash. Instead, he should have been
buying them. Even if he could have held them,
Berkshire should have made more money. J&J
stock doubled in value and P&G stock tripped,
not counting the dividends! Of course, Buffett
knew well of J&J and P&G's potential. Even
then, he sold shares in the hope of buying back
later.

I wonder why Wrigley fixed income at an 11.45% interest rate, while GE and Goldman fetched only 10% each? While, in the 2008 financial crash, the risk was more in GE and Goldman deals.

————

I have not come across any specific comment from Buffett about this deal.

Lessons:

1. A bear market is an opportunity to allocate capital 'extra' diligently to acquire shares in wonderful companies.

2. Investors need to understand deals with blurred boundaries. Facts matter more than feelings!

Chapter 31: Irish Banks
[Year – 2008]

Invest in a Specific Business Model.

In 2008, Buffett invested in two Irish banks (names unknown). These banks are involved in all kinds of land development loans. Ireland has a small geographical size and the population was less than 4.5 million in 2008.

Buffett identified these banks as "cheap" and invested a total of $244 million. These banks went into a downward spiral by the end of 2008. Buffett exited with an 89% loss and was able to recover only $27 million.

Buffett failed to understand the correct business mode of these banks. Land development loans have different business characteristics. In short, they differ from property loans. He got into a business without understanding the underlying business mode. Also, he miscalculated the potential dynamics of a business in Ireland.

———

Buffett's own words [2008 AR]:

"I was wrong on the Irish banks in a very big way. I simply didn't understand. And I should've understood. It was available for me to

understand, the incredible exposure they'd got into in more land development-type loans — not property loans, in terms of completed properties — but all kinds of land development loans... It was the terrible mistake by me. Nobody lied to me, nobody gave me any bad information. I just plain wasn't paying attention... The tennis crowd would call my mistakes 'unforced errors'."

Lessons:

1. There are various business models to make money and grow in a given industry. An investor needs to understand specifically a business model before investing.

2. The buy mistakes in a bear market cost more in terms of opportunity cost. These are occasions when an investor can buy more for a dollar.

Chapter 32: Derivative Contracts
[Year – 2008]

Need Blessing of Luck

In 2008, a volatile time, Berkshire wrote 251 derivative contracts. It received a $4.2 billion premium for them, considering them a 'float' type. During this time, Buffett saw concern in "equity put" contracts. He estimated these contracts as mostly mispriced at inception.

As of the 2023 AR, the investment and derivative gains were reported as $74.86 billion while in the last year, the losses topped $67.9 billion. These are mark-to-market or "paper" losses on the "put contracts". (Note: These include all contracts to date.) It was estimated that these contracts might give good returns. Two aspects played for Buffett here: 1) a comparative advantage during inception and 2) Luck!

I wonder about the fit for the Berkshire framework in the long term. *Do the new investment managers at Berkshire handle these complicated instruments?*

———

Buffett own words [2014 AR]:

"We have told you before that our derivative contracts, subject as they are to mark-to-market accounting, will produce wild swings in the earnings we report. The ups and downs neither cheer nor bother Charlie (Munger) and me."

"I believe each contract we own was mispriced at inception, sometimes dramatically so. I both initiated these positions and monitor them, a set of responsibilities consistent with my belief that the CEO of any large financial organization must be the chief risk officer as well. If we lose money on our derivatives, it will be my fault."

Lessons:

1. Risk management is pivotal for an investor in any transaction.

2. The role of luck in investment makes all the difference. There are two types of luck in investment: one, when preparation meets the opportunity and second, when an expected and unknown event brings positive surprises. This particular deal is the second type. God bless!

PART – C: Error of Omissions: "Thumb Sucking"

Warren Buffett's fabulous record for a long period makes him a great investor and businessman. Many people have mega investment returns, either for a short period or once in a while. However, having above-average returns over a lifetime, and not going broke sets him apart.

Buffett's biggest regrets were *"errors of omission"* or not investing in winners. These were the companies Buffett knew. He understood them and saw they would do well in the future, even though he did not choose to invest in them.

These mistakes all into the following broad categories:

1. Not buying
2. Bought, but in very small size
3. Bought late

The following are possible cases or scenarios for these mistakes:

a. The cases were not brought forth, even though the business potential was clear
b. The cases were started but buying stopped. He waited for the price to come back to the original price: a common syndrome investors face.

These errors of omission cases are interesting. Many of these companies were well within Buffett's *"circle of competence"*, but he did not act. Munger termed the behavior as *"sucking the thumb"*. He saw the opportunity but just kept observing and doing nothing. Fortunately, or unfortunately (?), these are mistakes not captured in the company accounting. Also, Berkshire shareholders and the public can't see them. In short, inaction cost Berkshire billions of dollars over time.

Buffett is a great learner, and very observant. He knew what was going on in business and the market. He knew many companies in the early stages that grew into giants later like Intel, Microsoft, and so forth. There are likely multiple reasons for skipping them for known reasons.

Buffett often says that many of the businesses he does not understand are out of his 'circle of competence'. We need to dissect a bit more to understand what he meant. He understood how these businesses work; however, he was not able to foresee how business economics would pan out in the future.

There could be many reasons for a lack of insight into the future. How the economics would pan out over a long period? What would be the competitive advantages? The 'moat' strength and durability. This might be due to the rapidly changing ecosystem dynamics and exposure to unforeseen catastrophes. The market disruptions. This makes picking a future winner '*hard*' for the particular businesses he deemed as "*out of his circle of competence*".

The obvious question comes to mind. Why invest in insurance given that it deals with uncertainty and unforeseen events? However, the crux of the game lies in how the contract is written. It relies on probabilistic scenarios and weights for occurrence. These parameters determine the premium so the chances of the insurance company having to compensate the insurer is near to *zero*. In this whole process, a "float" is accumulated for the owner's disposal.

Furthermore, Berkshire's size has grown so much that only a couple of companies could enter into the big insurance contracts. Low competition!

So, let's learn from the last part of the book and become a '*wiser investor*'.

———

Buffett's own words [ARs and AGMs]:

"We have been thumb-suckers at times with businesses that we understood well. And it may have been because we started buying, and the price moved up a little, and we waited around hoping we would get more at the price we

originally started — there could be a lot of things. But those are huge mistakes. Conventional accounting, of course, does not pick those up at all. But they're in our scorebook"

... "So the cost of that has been many, many billions. And I'll probably keep making that mistake. There are — the mistakes are made when there are businesses you can understand and they're attractive and you don't do something about it. I don't worry at all about the mistakes that come about because when I met Bill Gates, I didn't buy Microsoft or something. That's not my game. But the mistakes are made when you — most of our mistakes have been mistakes of omission rather than commission."

... "I made some errors of omission, sucking my thumb when new facts came in that should have caused me to re-examine my thinking and promptly take action."

... "Your chairman was a little reluctant to follow it, a terrible mistake... We've missed a lot of things. And I'm dead serious about that. And we've missed things that should not have been beyond our capacity to grasp. A lot of things that should be beyond our capacity to grasp, but there's some that haven't been. And we've just plain missed them."

Bonus: Charlie Munger's words [AR and AGMs]:

"The mistakes that have been most extreme in Berkshire's history are mistakes of omission. They don't show up in our figures. They show up in opportunity costs."

... "In other words, we have opportunities, we almost do it. In retrospect, we can tell that we were very much mistaken not to do it. In terms of the shareholders, those are the ones in our history that it really cost the most. And very few managements do much thinking or talking about opportunity costs. But , we have blown"

... "I think most people get very few, what I call, no-brainer opportunities, where it's just so damned obvious that this is going to work. And since they are very few and they may be separated by periods of years, I think people have to learn to have the courage and the intelligence to step up in a major way when those rare opportunities come by."

Chapter 33: Dallas-Fort Worth NBC Station
[Year 1972]

Learn The Art of Action and Inaction.

Fort Worth NBC had been running a TV station since 1948. The station had a different name then.

Tom Murphy ran Capital Cities Communication and planned to buy the Dallas-For-Worth NBC station. The Carter family owned it. The offer came with the Fort Worth paper. In 1974, the USA's Federal Communications Commission (FCC) made a ruling, prohibiting "cross-ownership" in the same region. Murphy turned to Buffett to sell the station for $35 million. Buffett didn't take the offer.

Murphy was Buffett's friend. He knew Buffett's investing style and was sure the Station would add value to Berkshire. Also, Buffett admired Murphy for his business acumen and character.

Buffett knew TV stations needed little capital to operate and would have an excellent future. Murphy himself was an expert in the station business and understood the ins and outs of it. In short, he offered future cash flows and assets to Buffett... but, Buffett just ignored it.

Fast forward to the 2007 Berkshire annual report: Buffett valued the property at $800 million. The station was earning $73 million before taxes and it earned up to $1 billion since he had turned down the offer.

———

Buffett's own words [2007 AR]:

"I knew that TV stations were See's-like businesses that required virtually no capital investment and had excellent prospects for growth. They were simple to run and showered cash on their owners... In effect Murph whispered "buy" into my ear. But I didn't listen... Why did I say "no"? The only explanation is that my brain had gone on vacation and forgot to notify me."

Lessons:

1. When an opportunity comes knocking, just act and grab it. It is as simple as that.

2. Take seriously the advice of someone you consider an expert and trust. Also, do your homework!

Chapter 34: Walmart Inc.
[Year- 1974]

Recognize Own Biases.

Walmart is a global retailer that Sam Walton started from scratch in 1962. Walmart is a giant. It operates worldwide in different formats: hypermarkets, discount stores, groceries, and e-commerce platforms.

Early on, Buffett recognized Walmart's good business model and potential. He planned to buy 100 million shares in the mid-1970s. Then the share price was $23 before the split. Munger too agreed to the investment in Walmart.

However, when Buffett started purchasing, the price started moving up. Buffett was not ready to purchase at a higher price even though knew of a bright future. The stock price did not fall, and Berkshire ended up purchasing a very small stake in it.

In Berkshire's 2014 annual report, Buffett confessed the mistake cost billions of dollars to Berkshire.

Later in 2005, Buffett began buying Walmart shares again. He kept buying until 2014. He acquired a 2.1% stake for approximately $3.8 billion, In 2014, the stake was valued at $5.8

billion. Walmart was in the top five common stock investments of Berkshire.

In 2015, Walmart cut future sales. This was because of wage increases and e-commerce investments. The share price plunged to $60 per share from about $90. During this time, from 2015 to 2017, Buffett completely sold all of his Walmart shares. When the share price was at a decade-low!

"Different types of mistakes. Now, I am running out of space to write. More about it, some later date…"

Buffett thought that the retail business was becoming tougher. Because of different types of competition e-commerce: Amazon.com. They were much ahead in technology platforms and revenue from it. He was finding it very hard to figure out the future winner. And he wanted to see around for easier games.

Fast forward to early 2024. The Walmart share price was about $180 per share. This was before the split in February 2024. During this time, Walmart's business did well. It also evolved to adapt to e-commerce. It has grown more worldwide and made a few acquisitions.

It is clear that Buffett undermined Walmart's operational strength. And he sold too soon. He could have waited for Walmart's response and come back. One possible reason for this sale was Amazon.com. Buffett admires Bezos's execution capabilities at Amazon. However, he miscalculated the impact on Walmart's business.

Walmart's revenue grew from $482 billion in 2016 to $611 in 2023; but the net profit dropped from $14.6 billion to $11.6 billion. Yet to see Walmart reaching its full potential.

———

Buffett's own words [2004 AGM]:

"Walmart — I cost us about — it's up to 10 billion now."

Bonus: Munger's own words [2004 AGM taking on Walmart's missed opportunity.]:

"At least we are constantly thinking about the past occasions when we blew opportunities. Since those don't hit financial reports, the opportunities you had but didn't accept, most people don't bother thinking about them very much. At least that is a mistake we don't make. We rub our own noses in our mistakes in blowing opportunities, as we just did."

[2017 AGM] *"We blew Walmart, too. When it was a total cinch, we were smart enough to figure that out and we didn't (act)."*

Lessons:

1. Investors must recognize their biases. They should not get trapped by price "anchoring" while buying. The long-term business potential needs to take precedence over the market price movement.

2. An investor needs thorough analysis before selling too. The way done during buy. Businesses need to adjust to new markets. Investors need to give time to understand reality and business impact. Also, how management is responding to the new scenarios. The market has no duty to understand your feelings.

Chapter 35: Google LLC (Alphabet Inc.)

[Year – 2004]

Upskill Technology Disruptions for Advantage.

Google is the most dominant search engine. The brand is synonymous with "search" on the Internet. It operates in the internet, cloud, advertising, software, hardware, and artificial intelligence domains.

Buffett knew Google from its early days. He and Berkshire owner's manual inspired Google's founders, Larry Page and Sergey Brin, to take the company public in 2004.

Buffett also knew about Berkshire's insurance subsidiary. GEICO was paying Google for every click. Berkshire was adding to Google's profit. Buffett had seen these advertisements are working. He had insights into business operations, and virtually no cost involved to run it.

As a principal, he stayed away from technology companies. He gave a miss to it. The opportunity cost billions to Berkshire. Both Buffett and Munger had seen the potential and witnessed the working of Google's ad business model. But, they did not act upon it. Not buying Google even after recognizing is a mistake!

PS: *Buffett got into Apple stock, not as a technology stock, but as a global digital consumer brand. Also, when Apple's valuation dropped to 10 times earnings. I see most people and media confused about it. Hence clarification here.*

———

Buffett's own words [2004 AGM]:

"If you buy into Google, having read their owner's manual, you know, you will — I think you'll know the kind of people you're associating with. You'll know what they will do and won't do."

Fast forward, [2018 AGM] *"We've looked at it, and you know, I made a mistake in not being able to come to a conclusion where I really felt that at the present prices that the prospects were far better than the prices indicated."*

Bonus: Munger's own words [2011 AGM, in the context of Google]:

"Well, I hate to admit this because I've ignored high-tech all my life, but I actually read that book "In the Plex" about Google, and I found it a very interesting book. And so here I am at my

advanced age, and I find it interesting the way people have created these engineering cultures, which are quite peculiar and different from most of what we have at Berkshire. And will I ever make any use of this? I doubt it. But I certainly enjoyed learning it. And if I enjoy learning it, I regard it as important, because I think that's what you're here for, is to go to bed every night a little wiser than you were when you got up."

[2017 AGM]: *"If you ask me, in retrospect, what was our worst mistake in the tech field, I think we were smart enough to figure out Google. Those ads worked so much better in the early days than anything else. So I would say that we failed you there. And we were smart enough to do it and didn't do it. We do that all the time, too."*

[2019 AGM]: *"We could see in our own operations how well that Google advertising was working. And we just sat there sucking our thumbs."*

Lessons:

1. Not to miss out on an investment opportunity where you are consuming their products and services. And you know they are minting money and have

the potential to scale up profitably.

2. We need to pay attention to our transactions and likes. The same, Peter Lynch emphasized on it.

3. In an ever-changing world, it is the norm now you come across newer business segments. Also, these businesses challenge existing incumbents. We as investors, face often dilemmas toward these newer opportunities. If some opportunities in which you believe and need less capital than produce might need to be considered. May a fraction of your capital to allocate. Of course, in consideration with other 'n' number of factors.

Chapter 36: Amazon.com Inc.
[Year - 2015]

Recognize the Power of New Enterprise's Dominance.

Amazon operates worldwide. It works in many domains, including e-commerce, cloud computing, online advertising, digital streaming, and artificial intelligence. It evolved over the last thirty years from selling books online to multiple product and service platforms.

Jeffrey Bezos (Jeff) started the company from his garage in 1994. In the last couple of decades, the company entered into many markets. Wherever Amazon entered, it disrupted that market and challenged the incumbent. For example, Amazon has been in a tug-of-war with age-old Walmart. In recent times, Amazon has become a battleground for revenue and profits.

Buffett was watching Amazon and Jeff's moves for a long time. Buffett understands a retaining business, and he was an admirer of Jeff's execution capabilities. He evaluated Amazon for its investment value.

However, Buffett failed to recognize the power of Amazon's business model and the agility demonstrated to dominate by scaling up. The model is powerful and disruptive in its respective market segments. But, Buffet undervalued the potential revenue growth; he always felt the quoted share price did not justify buying in.

The world is changing. Benjamin Graham's methods for valuation may need to *evolve* too; his principles have limitations in valuing new-age companies. It is the same trap Buffett got into. I believe the investment game is becoming *harder* now.

———

Buffett's own words [2016 interview]:

"Jeff Bezos has built an extraordinary economic machine from standing still, a start of zero, with competitors with lots of capital.... I should have bought (Amazon) long ago, but I didn't understand the power of the model and the price always seemed more than the power of the model. I missed big time,"

[2018 AGM]: *"I made the wrong decision on Google. And Amazon, I just — I really consider that a miracle, that you could be doing Amazon web services and changing retail at the same time, with — you know, without enormous amounts of capital, and with the speed and effectiveness of what Amazon has done. I just —*

I underestimated — I had a very, very, very high opinion of Jeff's ability when I first met him. And I underestimated him"

Lessons:

1. Asset-based and Discounted Cash Flow (DCF) valuation techniques have their limitations. The same techniques could not be applied to all businesses.

2. Business value now is in selling solutions to customers so they not only stick to the business but also cross-sell a variety of other products and services. Technological advances and innovations are changing business landscapes faster than ever. Customers are constantly hunting for better buying experiences. The scenarios are becoming tougher for investors to judge. It's hard to look at a 7-8 year horizon!

3. The ability of management to thrive through rapid changes matters more than ever. They must do so with a single focus on returns to owners.

Chapter 37: Pharma Companies
[Year - 1993]

Candidate for the 'Basket Investment' Style.

Bill Clinton was elected president of the United States in 1993. He started work on a healthcare reform plan. The people felt the need for regulation to curb drug prices. Pharma stocks were beaten down.

Both Buffett and Munger understood the pharma industry. They knew the industry was important to humanity. Buffett concluded that, in the future, drug companies would have a much higher return on equity.

During this time, Buffett started buying Johnson & Johnson, a big pharma company; but he stopped shortly after, as the stock price rose. In fact, Berkshire could have bought *the whole pharma industry* at this time. Buffett admitted this was a mistake. In 1997, at Berkshire's annual meeting, Buffett confessed, saying he had ignored pharma companies for investments.

Buffett highlighted one issue for not buying pharma. He was not able to distinguish a specific pharma company that would succeed in the future, although he understood the industry and its potential.

In my view, in these scenarios, you see the business potential but can't pick the winner. So, you use the *'basket investment'* approach. You may buy dominant companies when they have shown profitability, and you believe in the management.

PS: *Lately, in 2020, Berkshire has made few pharma investments. However, I could not verify, if Buffett or other Berkshire managers had made them. Hence no comments.*

———

Buffett's own words [1997 AGM]:

"The pharmaceutical industry is, obviously, been a terrific industry to invest in. We have trouble, or at least I have trouble, distinguishing among the companies, in terms of seeing which ones, ten years from now, might be the best ones to be in.

I mean, it's easy for me to figure out that Coca-Cola's the soft drink company to be in, or Gillette is the shaving company to be in, or Disney's the entertainment company to be in, than it is for me to figure out which one in the pharmaceutical. But that — I'm not saying you can't do it. I'm just saying that that's difficult for me.

We have — we started buying one of them a couple of years ago. And we should've continued, but we didn't because it went up an eighth. Your chairman was a little reluctant to follow it, a terrible mistake.

But I would say the biggest — and we could've bought the whole industry and done very well at various times, particularly when the threat of — what people thought was the threat of the Clinton health program cast a big cloud over the pharmaceutical industry.

That was the time you could've just bought the whole industry and done very well. We didn't do it. It was a mistake."

Bonus: Munger's own words [1997 AGM]:

"Well, it's hard to think of any industry that's done more good for consumers, generally. When you think of the way children used to die and now, they very seldom die. And it's been a fabulous business. And it's been one of the glories of American civilization. But it's — we've admired it. But we haven't been part of it."

Lessons:

1. Investors should be aware of their own biases.

2. Some basics to successful investing: 1) Seize the opportunity when it arrives; 2) Size up the opportunity; 3) If the opportunity is growing in the future, do not wait for the price to come down to an earlier price (i.e., avoid "price anchoring") and 4) Limit economic news interference in the decision as long as you see value with a margin-of-safety.

3. Avoid anchoring to the initial price of purchasing a stock. Give more weight to business performance and potential, if your purchase thesis is still intact. As growth becomes more visible, it attracts more investors, and market prices are pushed upward. A wise investor should embrace it, as she or he is riding on the right boat.

4. In a scenario where you understand an industry's potential but can't pick the winner, go by the 'basket investment' approach. You buy companies you believe would be in the winning category and you comfort with their management. You may treat this as an industry-specific index fund investing.

5. I recommend to build a wider toolkit in
    investment to use one as opportunity
    demand. It would help to evolve and
    bring more choices.

Chapter 38: Tobacco Industry
[Year 1989]

Profit vs Ethics.

"You must remember that some things legally right are not morally right." - Abraham Lincoln

As you are aware tobacco products are addictive and consumers are loyal to a brand. Buffett understood the tobacco business and knew he could make tons of money. His thesis was, *"A penny to make a cigarette and sell it for a dollar"*.

R. J. Reynolds Nabisco Inc. (RJR Nabisco) a US-based conglomerate was in the business of tobacco and food products. In 1988, the company was taken over by Kohiberg Kravis Roberts & Co. (KKR) in the largest leveraged buyout in history then for $25 billion.

Post KKR takeover, in 1989, RJR Nabisco bonds had been bitten heavily. Buffett found it a valuable opportunity, so he bought bonds worth $440 million. Later, in 1991, he sold the bonds for a gain of $150 million. Later years, Buffett clarified that he might like to buy tobacco stocks as a value buy, although he does not prefer to own the whole business as the tobacco business is burdened with taxation and other moral issues.

*****

Many of Berkshire investment companies were involved in the distribution of tobacco products: for examples as Walmart, and PriceCostco (earlier holdings). Also, the newspapers carried tobacco product advertisements. Buffett found tobacco businesses attractive for investment, although he had not bought significantly in recent times. He skipped investing in a chewing tobacco company that later did well.

PS: *I included it because tobacco businesses were in Buffett's circle of competence. He was interested but did not buy. At the 2021 AGM, Buffett and Munger confirmed that a few years ago, they declined a profitable opportunity to invest in a tobacco-related product... and it was not as harmful as other tobacco products.*

———

Buffett's own words [1997 AGM]:

"We have owned — we won't comment on what we own now — but we have owned tobacco stocks in the past. We've never owned a lot of them, although we may have made a mistake by not owning a lot of them. But we've owned tobacco stocks in the past... The fact that we've not been significant holders of tobacco stocks has not been because they've been on a boycotted list with us. It just means that overall

we were uncomfortable enough about their prospects over time that we did not feel like making a big commitment in them."

Bonus: Munger's own words [1997 AGM]:

"I think each company, each individual, has to draw its own ethical and moral lines, and personally, I like the messy complexity of having to do that. It makes life interesting."

Lessons:

1. Few industries are good as investments. But there is a thin line between capitalism and ethical social causes.

2. Investors need to take their calls on this. Are they willing to own this kind of business for profit?

Note: *In the early stage of my investment journey in 2005, I invested ("traded: is a better word) in a leading Indian tobacco company. I soon sold out with a profit. Later, I traded in alcoholic beverage companies and profited. I recently stopped considering them for my investments for ethical reasons. I trust, there is no shortage of investment opportunities in other industries!*

In Conclusion

Embrace Mistakes. Embrace Learning. Stay in The Game.

A *wise* investor quickly acknowledges the mistakes that she or he makes; it shows their *humility*. It also shows their confidence to rise again gracefully. Mistakes are part and parcel of the investment journey. The key is to learn from these mistakes, preferably from other people.

The major learnings from Buffett's investment journey are as follows:

1. Understand the economic characteristics and long-term sustainable competitive advantage.
2. Value the business's future prospects.
3. Be philosophical about market price movements and guard your biases.
4. Act decisively.
5. Let go, if missed opportunities.
6. Have a feedback system in place to keep a check and **evolve**.

Learning and staying in the game is what matters over a period of time. The same thing worked for Buffett and Berkshire beautifully, even after making all sorts of mistakes and errors. The most important lesson to be learned from Buffett's journey are: ***you don't need to be right all the time. Even if you make a few right decisions that would change your life.***

It is so overwhelming that all negatives do not get counted. Investing as a lifestyle is fascinating, offering many opportunities to learn. Here, ***the learning is multidimensional: personal discovery, business economics, value framework, and how the world works.***

This quest for broader learning and fun made me move from a technocrat to an investor.

It is important in this ever-changing world to learn and keep upgrading our understanding day by day. This *habit* gives us more and bigger opportunities in the marketplace. The vital part of the investment game is to ***play, learn, and evolve.*** I am sure that the whole process prepares you to make wiser decisions to recognize the opportunities. When your preparation meets an opportunity, it is called ***luck!***

Become a seeker of luck through your conscious efforts, and train your subconscious mind for the same. With

this, I trust that you will succeed. This not only helps you excel in finances but also makes you live a more joyful and fulfilled Life!

———

Final Words from the Masters:

Buffett's own words: *"Part of making good decisions in business is recognizing the poor decisions you've made and why they were poor. I've made lots of mistakes. I'm going to make more. It's the name of the game. You don't want to expect perfection in yourself. You want to strive to do your best. It's too demanding to expect perfection in yourself."*

"You only have to do a very few things right in your life so long as you don't do too many things wrong."

Bonus Munger's own words: *"We are very stupid in many ways, but we have avoided a slight subset of stupidities. And they're important."*

"Nothing to Add."

Full Book Lessons

PART - A

Chapter 1: Berkshire Hathaway Inc.

1. An investor needs to be close to the matter to be rational. The facts matter rather than being carried away by emotions. The market doesn't know about either your feelings or emotions.

2. The key to investing is to understand why something is "cheaply" available. Is It really an opportunity for long term journey or just a cigar butt?

3. The cigar-butt investment style has a classic challenge. It looks only at the gap between market price and intrinsic value and misses the big picture. It's a short-sighted approach that might work in trading of marketable securities; however, not as a long-term investor or as a business owner. To gain long term, you need to know the business's economic traits.

4. Investors need to remain agile and recognize their circle of competence.

They need to book losses or bad investments as quickly as possible. It not only frees up capital but also the mental capital to focus on other better investment opportunities. In the span of twenty years, Buffett recognized that the textile business would not generate high returns on investments. However, he delayed and hoped for a reasonable return.

5. If the investor's thesis has broken, she or he should reevaluate the scenarios and plan to sell sooner rather than later to free-up the resources.

Chapter 2: Waumbec Textile Company

1. The commodity businesses' consolidation and synergy strategies fail faster to historic average or below. Here, 1+1 is less than 2.

2. Cigar-butt value investing is a trading strategy. However, if you are investing for the long-term, you need to avoid them for three reasons. First, they eat up capital. Second, the time to realize the gain is unknown. Third, holding them burns out investor's mental resources and other better opportunities.

3. It is always a wise idea to correct a mistake as early as possible rather than hoping for better days.

Chapter 3: Hochschild Kohn & Co.

1. A business owner needs to evaluate its sustainable competitive strength to operate and produce profits.

2. Merely engaging in an acquisition solely based on asset price lacks a rationale, unless the acquisition is pursued with the intention to liquidate for profit.

Chapter 4: National Indemnity Company

1. Ownership and capital structure are the starting point for any investment journey. The percentage of your holding in a business decides the long-term economic benefits you gain from it.

2. Once you pick up an investment vehicle, changing later can be expensive and hard. So, plan capital structure and allocation with an eye to future plans to maximize the gains.

Chapter 5: The Walt Disney Company

1. Long-term compounding in wonderful businesses works like magic. So, sit tight on them. Conversely, selling wonderful business too soon is a mistake.

2. Before making any investment decision, specifically on selling, weigh it critically Here you are juggling among potential business prospectus, market scenarios, and opportunity costs.   Hence selling is tricky in the investment business.

3. Selling makes sense if the original reason to buy is no longer valid. This could be due to fundamental challenges in business growth. Or, the share price might have risen unrealistically high, and *valuations* are not justified. Or, you might get a better opportunity.

Chapter 6: Capital Cities/ABC Inc.

1. An investor's job is not only to buy and hold but also to track the business and industry prospects. The opportunity cost to hold or sell could be a better decision criteria, rather than "permanence'"

2. The permanent investment holding is *a myth*. The world is changing faster than

ever. Businesses have faced consistent challenges from technological innovations and changes in customer preferences.

Chapter 7: Nebraska Furniture Mart

1. A well-drafted formal contract helps in any business deal, to avoid any unforeseen and unpleasant surprises in the future.

2. The promoter(s) and their family dynamics make a lot of difference for a family run business. It decides not only the business' fate but also the shareholders' treatment.

Chapter 8: World Book Inc.

1. Personal computers and the Internet changed the world and the way businesses operate since the 1990s. This was a titanic shift in world order. In investing, one must recognize disruptions and handle their affairs well.

2. New technologies are bringing rapid changes to the world and to businesses. An investor's job is getting harder to

identify the businesses with lasting competitive advantages.

3. Shying away from understanding newer technology and its impact on business is no longer an option in this era. To stay and grow in the investment game, you need to keep learning and act based on newer facts.

Chapter 9: USAir Group Inc.

1. The insight into the nature of business is crucial for investment. A more critical approach to the margin of safety is needed for commodities like businesses.

2. For long-term investment success, you need to look for a lasting competitive edge.

3. I see many investors become carried away by sales growth (top-line). However, investors and smart businessmen need to *demand* growing retained earnings.

4. The cost analysis to run a business is part of the basic hygiene check. The real test is the requirement for external capital to grow.

Chapter 10: Salomon Brothers Inc.

1. In the financial world, **trust** is most important in any transaction. It cultivates creditability and a lifelong reputation. An investor needs to demand from the people who are running the business. My grandmother used to say *that earning a reputation takes a lifetime, but you can lose it in a moment.*

2. It is wise to avoid an investment if you do not have insight into the future business prospects and profitability. Hence, need an edge.

3. Even if you trust the management based on past behavior, you need to be vigilant about their affairs.

Chapter 11: Dexter Shoe Company

1. In a global scenario where goods can be moved easily across borders, it makes competition more severe where everyone seeks low-cost opportunities. This is far truer for unregulated commodity businesses.

2. Overconfidence and the thrill of past successes are the enemy of an investor.

3. In the long run, equity is always costly compared to cash. Hence, as an investor, you need to have a sharp focus on the issuance of shares in different forms: ESOPs, Warrants, Preferential, and Share swaps in acquisitions. These will dilute your ownership and per-share business value. Hence, these share offers need to be analyzed critically and weighted against future prospectus. I avoided many companies where negligence occurs in share issuance.

Chapter 12: McDonald's Corporation

1. Few brands travel the world easily. The beauty lies in the standardized setup and processes to create an identity in the consumer's experience.

2. These businesses are worth holding for long-term capital appreciation and dividends.

3. A successful investor acts when required and makes money from inactivity. Inactivity is understated in the investment world.

4. Involvement in the hyperactive often breeds mistakes.

Chapter 13: Buying 2% in Silver

1) To succeed in commodity, a trader needs to know the market. This means supply-and-demand scenarios, and the discipline to wait for a chance to trade.

2) An equity investor might trade commodities as a hobby. They do it to take once-a-while advantage of changes in supply and demand.

Chapter 14: Costco Wholesale Corporation

1. An investor loads up on the shares of a company within his or her circle of competence.

2. Selling a wonderful business based on price movement is not an investment (business-like). It's a trading strategy.

Chapter 15: General Reinsurance Corporation

1. Diluting equity should be a last resort for a "mature" and "responsible" company. An investor could consider it in the framework while deciding on an investment.

2. We need to understand a peculiar fact about equity. Once issued, it stays on a company's books unless bought back. Reversing these equity dilutions is tough and many times costly to reverse. But if the same transaction is done in cash or through debt, it could have been easily fixed by paying with operating cash.

3. In investing, I look for the company's equity issuance "habits". If a company issues ESOPs or dilutes for expansions, I consider them in the evaluation process. This is not seen as widely used.

4. Any kind of desperation to act is an investment mistake.

5. The investigation is vital in investment. It is basic to understand past events and their impacts on future business affairs. And we are investing for the future!

6. Evaluating Management is a tricky part. An investor needs to study past behavior. They also need to watch for future actions.

Chapter 16: PetroChina Company Ltd.

1. Selling in the market is tricky to avoid regrets or overwhelming feelings. The weighing on risk probabilities needs a well-defined investment framework. It helps to address both facets of opportunity to gain, and probability of loss on the judgement day of transaction.
2. As the capital base balloons, the opportunity size shrinks for an investor. It is tough situation to manage performance and the risk.

Chapter 17: Energy Future Holdings Corp.

1. Global energy prices are usually tied to supply and demand. Gas prices stay high or rise unidirectional was the assumption, so the investment was a mistake. In fact it was a trade.

2. An investor needs to watch out for higher valuations in a bull market, specifically.

It is even more crucial for businesses operating in commodities or/and are regulated.

3. Invert, always invert' the scenarios to have a robust investment framework.

Chapter 18: ConocoPhillips Company

1. Investing in oil and gas requires understanding their cycles. Many things affect prices, including cycles in regional and global economies. Also, consider geopolitical events and transportation scenarios.

2. Nothing new: don't try to time the market!

3. As always, an investor needs to watch out for euphoria within, and then outside on Wall Street. Act only when needed to your advantage.

4. 'Invert, always invert.' It is your thesis to get better insights.

5. 'Opportunity cost' is one of the basic matrices used in allocating capital. In the 2008 market crash, capital could be used well for beaten-down, attractive stocks.

Chapter 19: TESCO Plc.

1. Selling in the market is tricky; it demands emotional stability. It pays to be philosophical about selling to avoid regret if prices rise.

2. A wise investor is disciplined. She or he does things their way, based on a framework and process. They act immediately in a controlled way when the original buy thesis fails. I may write more about selling one day.

3. For a retailer to expand, many things must fall in place. These include cheap procurement, efficient distribution, wide sales pricing strategies, and grow loyal customers. It gets complicated because of local and global market dynamics and competition. The competition is among local stores, discount stores, and mega-retailers. It is a tough business.

4. We need to recheck the thesis with any changes in key management as it might lead to changes in business models and the company culture.

Chapter 20: NetJets Inc.

1. Some businesses suck in too much capital to expand. It demands external capital, either using debt or equity. As they are unable to produce sufficient retained earnings.

2. Investors need to watch out for real owner's earnings over longer periods. Few traders take advantage of expansion announcements. However, this strategy might work for a short duration with its limitations.

3. Not all subscription businesses that collect advance money from customers will succeed. The underlines business economics take precedence.

4. Having the right management is crucial. They must have an ownership mind-set. This is key for equity investors.

Chapter 21: International Business Machine Corp. (IBM)

1. A disciplined investor stays in their own circle of competence. She or he understands its boundaries and honors

them.

2. The key criteria for an investment is the business's long-term competitive edge so it can deliver satisfactory returns to the owners.

3. It is a BIG challenge for investors in an ever-changing technological world. Investing is becoming more complex as more and more brain power is getting dedicated to it.

4. Share repurchases and dividends are important in an investment theme; however, business performance needs to lead them.

Chapter 22: Lubrizol Corporation

1. An investor needs to have insight into the nature of the business and its economic character. A chemical business is competitive and governed by many environmental laws. Plus, it is exposed to innovations and market disruptions.

2. Insight into management behavior is challenging. As investors, we need to deal with it.

3.   One way is to look at how management
     had behaved in the past. Are there any
     red flags in the operation of the business?
     Also, it was vital to understand the
     treatment given to the shareholders.

Chapter 23: The Kraft Heinz Company

1.   The food and beverages market is
     becoming more competitive, as big
     retailers are pushing their private
     brands.

2.   Real brand power commands a top price.
     It dictates pricing to distributors and
     retailers. Of course, the customer's pull is
     strong.

3.   Even power brand images drift over time
     and ease bargaining power. Investors
     need to consider more challenges for
     these companies. E-commerce is rising,
     and goods move faster. Meanwhile,
     valuing them became a regular exercise.

4.   For investors, overpaying causes two
     issues: a) upward potential gets limited
     and b) opportunity cost.

Chapter 24: Precision Castparts Corp. (PCC)

1. Valuation is the key that decides the investor's gain over time. *"Price what you pay; value what you get."*

2. The casting and forging industry is competitive. Customers prefer a couple of suppliers and play around for better deals.

3. These companies get squeezed among customers, raw material suppliers, and labor. Everyone wants to take a larger share of the profit.

Chapter 25: Newspapers (Print Media)

1. An investor should never say "never". There is nothing like permanence in business and in life.

2. An investor needs to be agile to act quickly when the original story breaks down, rather than be carried away by denial bias.

3. Generally, doing a transaction purely for tax advantages might be a mistake.

Chapter 26: Manufacturing, Service and Retailing Operations

1. The acquisitions with goodwill and other intangible assets make sense when they bring more cash-generating power to the company.

2. An investor needs to scrutinize these acquisitions given the benefits to the owner for the premium paid. Furthermore, watch out for the treatment given to them and the possibility of a write-off in the future.

Chapter 27: Taiwan Semiconductor Manufacturing Company Ltd. (TSMC)

1. Having a business in a single region or distributed across the globe brings its own challenges. The concentration of risk comes with efficiency and less overhead costs. While having operations spread across many locations brings other sets of challenges. The company needs to open a new facility and maintain it. Plus, it will need to follow different regional laws and cultures. It must also deal with currency fluctuations, logistics, and the availability of skilled labor and

administrative resources.

2. If an investor finds a wonderful business with a long-term competitive advantage, operated by able and trusted people and available at a price that you like, then it is time to seize the opportunity.

3. Future events are uncertain, and an investor needs to take a judgmental view. Given the risks and rewards, the investor always needs to factor in capital allocation.

<h2 style="text-align:center"><u>PART – B</u></h2>

Chapter 28: General Electric Corporation (GE)

1. Whenever you hear management talking about diversification, you need to become alert.
    I ran away from financial companies that talked about 'innovation in finances and products'.

2. As an investor, you need to decide when, where, and how much money to leave on the table.

Chapter 29: The Goldman Sachs Group Inc.

1.   Understandably, businesses are done with personal relationships. However, as an investor, watch out for the intent behind the transactions.

2.   In a depressed stock market, getting into a fixed-price deal is most likely a bad idea.

Chapter 30: Wrigley Company

1.   A bear market is an opportunity to allocate capital 'extra' diligently to acquire shares in wonderful companies.

2.   Investors need to understand deals with blurred boundaries. Facts matter more than feelings!

Chapter 31: Irish Banks

1.   There are various business models to make money and grow in a given industry. An investor needs to understand specifically a business model

before investing.

2. The buy mistakes in a bear market cost more in terms of opportunity cost. These are occasions when an investor can buy more for a dollar.

Chapter 32: Derivative Contracts

1. Risk management is pivotal for an investor in any transaction.
2. The role of luck in investment makes all the difference. There are two types of luck in investment: one, when preparation meets the opportunity and second, when an expected and unknown event brings positive surprises. This particular deal is the second type. God bless!

<u>PART – C</u>

Chapter 33: Dallas-Fort Worth NBC Station

1. When an opportunity comes knocking, just act and grab it. It is as simple as that.

2. Take seriously the advice of someone you consider an expert and trust. Also, do your homework!

Chapter 34: Walmart Inc.

1. Investors must recognize their biases. They should not get trapped by price "anchoring" while buying. The long-term business potential needs to take precedence over the market price movement.

2. An investor needs thorough analysis before selling too. The way done during buy. Businesses need to adjust to new markets. Investors need to give time to understand reality and business impact. Also, how management is responding to the new scenarios. The market has no duty to understand your feelings.

Chapter 35: Google LLC (Alphabet Inc.)

1. Not to miss out on an investment opportunity where you are consuming their products and services. And you know they are minting money and have

the potential to scale up profitably.

2. We need to pay attention to our transactions and likes. The same, Peter Lynch emphasized on it.

3. In an ever-changing world, it is the norm now you come across newer business segments. Also, these businesses challenge existing incumbents. We as investors, face often dilemmas toward these newer opportunities. If some opportunities in which you believe and need less capital than produce might need to be considered. May a fraction of your capital to allocate. Of course, in consideration with other 'n' number of factors.

Chapter 36: Amazon.com Inc.

1. Asset-based and Discounted Cash Flow (DCF) valuation techniques have their limitations. The same techniques could not be applied to all businesses.

2. Business value now is in selling solutions to customers so they not only stick to the business but also cross-sell a variety of other products and services. Technological advances and innovations

are changing business landscapes faster than ever. Customers are constantly hunting for better buying experiences. The scenarios are becoming tougher for investors to judge. It's hard to look at a 7-8 year horizon!

3. The ability of management to thrive through rapid changes matters more than ever. They must do so with a single focus on returns to owners.

Chapter 37: Pharma Companies

1. Investors should be aware of their own biases.

2. Some basics to successful investing: 1) Seize the opportunity when it arrives; 2) Size up the opportunity; 3) If the opportunity is growing in the future, do not wait for the price to come down to an earlier price (i.e., avoid "price anchoring") and 4) Limit economic news interference in the decision as long as you see value with a margin-of-safety.

3. Avoid anchoring to the initial price of purchasing a stock. Give more weight to business performance and potential, if your purchase thesis is still intact. As

growth becomes more visible, it attracts more investors, and market prices are pushed upward. A wise investor should embrace it, as she or he is riding on the right boat.

4. In a scenario where you understand an industry's potential but can't pick the winner, go by the *'basket investment'* approach. You buy companies you believe would be in the winning category and you comfort with their management. You may treat this as an industry-specific index fund investing.

5. I recommend to build wider toolkit in investment to use one as opportunity demand. It would help to evolve and bring more choices.

Chapter 38: Tobacco Industry

1. Few industries are good as investments. But there is a thin line between capitalism and ethical social causes.

2. Investors need to take their calls on this. Are they willing to own this kind of business for profit?

Definitions

- **AGM:** Berkshire Hathaway Annual General Meeting. Unless otherwise specified.

- **AR:** Annual Report of Berkshire Hathaway Inc. unless otherwise specified.

- **Owner:** Who owns a piece of the business by holding the stocks.

- **Businessman:** A person who enjoys owning the business, and doing all the activities to carry out affairs to get maximum economic as well as personal satisfaction (fulfillment).

- **Investor:** A person who intends to make rational decisions based on facts and the prospectuses of marketable securities by paying the price and, in return, expects to get value over a reasonable period.

- **Scuttlebutt investor:** An investor carries out the research of a company to invest by gathering information from on

the ground: employees, customers,
suppliers, and other sources.

- **Cigar-butt investor:** A trader trying to
  take advantage of the gap between
  market price and perceived value of the
  company (typically based on liquidating
  value).

- **Trader:** Follows the pure philosophy of
  buying low and selling high irrespective
  of underlines business/asset/securities
  irrespective of time of the day or week.
  For her or him the price is everything.

- **Speculator:** A speculator, operates as a
  trader with few conceived past beliefs,
  environment, and hopes to gain *always*
  in any market.

- **Marketable securities:** Equity, bonds,
  and similar means that could be traded
  in the marketplace.

- **Berkshire:** Berkshire Hathaway Inc.

- **ESOPs:** Employee Stock Option (or
  Ownership) Plans

- **Float:** The money an insurer holds
  between receiving the premium upfront
  and paying the claims later. A "collect-

now, pay-later" model could be applied in subscription-based businesses, in derivative 'option writers' and so forth.

- **$:** US dollar

- **£:** UK pound

Bibliography

My Gratitude.

- https://www.berkshirehathaway.com/
- https://www.nasdaq.com/
- https://www.nyse.com/index
- https://en.wikipedia.org/wiki/Main_Page
- https://Buffett.cnbc.com/
- https://www.businessinsider.com/
- https://www.fool.com/
- https://www.ft.com/
- **Respective companies' websites**

"The Intelligent Investor's" Book Series

"Be a learning machine to evolve to achieve your maximum potential and dreams."

I am writing **"The Intelligent Investor's"** as a series of books to help you in your investment journey. These are niche topics and no-nonsense.

Book No. 1:

The Intelligent Investor's Mistakes: Warren Buffett

The book you read.

Book No. 2:

The Intelligent Investor's Approach to Risk Mastery

This book is probably the first holistic risk mastery.

The book was the **#1 New Release** on a leading USA platform in the Risk Management and Mutual Funds categories.

In investment, the risk is inevitable, but its severity and probability vary. The book empowers you to manage the risk to - *1) minimize the losses and 2) weigh the opportunity cost to maximize Profits.* Further, you can devise the framework and strategies to take on long-term investment success.

The book is divided into four parts –

1. **Transform your mindset** and emotional intelligence to master effective investment decisions.
2. **Dive deep into business and industry ecosystems** to determine long-term compounding cash flows.
3. **Empower you to choose the exceptional management** to care for your ownership interest.
4. **Recognize your edge to stand out from the crowd mentality** to spot profitable investments and trading opportunities.

Get the Access Now:

1. Amazon Platform:
   https://relinks.me/B0DF1M8V7L

QR-Scan:

2. Apple Books:
   https://rxe.me/6689522091

3. Other Platforms:
   https://books2read.com/u/m2alod

4. Audio Book @Kobo Walmart:
   https://shorturl.at/P1O8Q

Book No. 3:

The Intelligent Investor's Art of Selling

Investors lose their potential fortunes in the stock market because of wrong selling. Understanding this is critical.

Selling in the stock market is **riskier, harder, requires strategy, and is an art.** But you will realize *real profits only when you sell successfully.*

This book is *your roadmap to mastering the sell strategies* in the stock market. Inside, you'll learn how to:

1. Identify and bust common myths about selling.
2. Break free from emotional biases and develop a resilient investor mindset.
3. Craft your personal *'why'* and *'when' to sell* to make effective decisions.
4. Confidently *take profits using a set of holistic, time-tested selling rules.*

Empower yourself with the strategies to secure profits on your path to lasting wealth. Selling is the ultimate skill every investor must master.

Remember:

"Selling is riskier than buying, but those who understand it build enduring wealth in the stock market."

Get the access now:

1. Amazon Platform:
   https://relinks.me/B0DLMDGRY4

   QR-Scan: 

2. Apple Books:
   https://relinks.me/6737729733

3. Other Platforms:
   https://books2read.com/u/4DqWed

4. Audio Book @Kobo Walmart:
   https://shorturl.at/PgWIz

The Intelligent Investors Hub

A community for you to learn investing to build enduring wealth.

Highlights:

1. **Learn:** Courses, live sessions and one-to-one coaching to mater the Stock market.
2. **Implement:** Own framework and strategies that suit you based on your own goals and risk appetites. In hackathon sessions you design own and get ideas on most important aspects of investments.
3. **Collaborate:** The community is a safe place to share and take a peaceful investment journey.

We understand the journey towards financial freedom is long. Hence, the membership is for a lifetime.

To explore The Intelligent Investors Hub Community visit us at:

www.intelligentinvestorshub.com

Scan QR Code:

*****